Instructor's Notes

Everything's an Argument with Readings

Instructor's Notes

Everything's an Argument with Readings

Sixth Edition

Andrea A. Lunsford
John J. Ruszkiewicz
Keith Walters

Prepared by John Kinkade, Jodi Egerton,
and Taryne Hallett

Bedford/St. Martin's
Boston ◆ New York

8   7   6   5   4   3
f   e   d   c   b   a

For information, write: Bedford/St. Martin's, 75 Arlington Street, Boston, MA 02116   (617-399-4000)

ISBN: 978-1-4576-0926-8

Contents

Chapter 24: Why Worry about Food and Water? 105

Making a Visual Argument: Apples to Oranges 110

Chapter 25: What Should "Diversity on Campus" Mean and Why? 128

Making a Visual Argument: Student-Designed Diversity Posters 129

Introduction

The title *Everything's an Argument* represents our conviction that all language is *motivated*. Because language is a human activity and because humans exist in a complex world of goals, purposes, and activities, language cannot be anything *but* motivated. In the words of Kenneth Burke, whose work has been central to the conception of this text, language is a form of "symbolic action": it gets things done in the world, acting on people and situations. The weak version of this argument claims simply that language has effects in the world or that people use language to accomplish ends; most of us would have no difficulty accepting that proposition.

But we hold to the strong version of the argument, maintaining, with Burke, that all language is *inherently* a form of argument. In this formulation of the claim, people use language to create *identification* between themselves and their audience. We cannot escape this naturally human function of language. The flip side of the argument that all language is motivated is powerful, too: all language is open to interpretation and negotiation. Production and analysis of language in this model require not just reason but also all the sensory faculties and an awareness of the rhetor's and the audience's history and experiences. Burke's definition of language's scope and power makes apparently simple activities—chatting with friends, reading the newspaper, writing a note to yourself—into scenes of argument and identification. We are all "wordlings," made of language as much as users of it.

In *A Grammar of Motives*, Burke introduced the dramatistic pentad, a way of describing the human uses of language and the relationships among people, their language, and their world. The five elements—act, scene, agent, agency, purpose—do not appear explicitly in this text, but the concepts remain important to us. The text's focus on the ethical problems of language use reflects our sense that responsible argument always considers the rhetorical situation in all its fullness; without attention to the ethical positions writers and readers inhabit, rhetoric—productive *and* analytic—is irresponsible. We hope that this text will help students learn to use language well, as readers and as writers, and that students will come to understand the complex role language plays in their life and world.

A Note on Teaching Strategy

If there's one strategy that we recommend above all others, it's using models to illustrate how arguments work and what you value in student writing. The book contains great samples of each kind of argument, but we think you can never have too many. When you find an article that clearly illustrates a definition or causal or evaluation argument, save it. When a student turns in an excellent paper, ask for his or her permission to save a copy to use as an example in future classes (we've found that most students are flattered by the request and happy to agree). It's great to build in a class period or two about a week before a paper is due to go over samples of what you consider good writing; if you have a rubric, have students read the papers with the rubric beside them so that they can practice applying your standards. We also recommend that you keep a file folder that has enough copies of sample arguments for everyone in your class (or ready access to an electronic copy if you can project readings in class), so that on those days when you're running short on planning time, or when your teaching plans go faster than you thought and you have extra time, you have an activity ready to go.

Notes for Using the Readings

You've probably already noticed that the anthology of readings in *Everything's an Argument with Readings* is quite different from the collections of readings in other rhetoric texts. Consistent with the title of the book, the readings include traditional essays as well as arguments in other genres—newspaper articles, poems, cartoons, Web sites, and more. Some genres may be unfamiliar at first, but we hope you will discover, as we have, that the variety gives you a great deal of flexibility and allows you to approach argumentation from fresh perspectives that can help your students readily grasp the value of rhetoric in its real-life applications.

Each chapter's readings contain at least one traditional essay that can serve as a model of the kind of writing that students are learning to produce. News pieces can be especially valuable for helping students learn to identify authors' points of view, even in contexts where the writer's stance isn't overtly stated. In the Respond exercises following each reading, students may be asked to find and state the positions taken in the journalistic pieces, or they may be asked to redraft an argument into academic essay format. Such exercises have a threefold purpose—to test comprehension, to assist students in understanding the importance of style and tone in various genres, and to give students practice in crafting academic prose. An additional value of these exercises is that they incorporate ideas and conclusions already provided by the reading, thereby enabling students to focus strictly on the craft of writing.

The chapter topics were chosen for their currency in public discourse and for their complexity. None of them can be considered a simple pro/con question or a clear-cut issue of conventional conservative/liberal opposition. We expect one of the benefits of this variety to be that the alliances among students in your classroom discussions throughout the term will shift with the various topics, allowing students to both acquaint themselves with a broader range of ideas and find commonality with a broader range of people than they might otherwise. The readings within each chapter contribute to that complexity both by their content and by the variety of genres and media represented.

The exercises following the readings are quite varied, although there is at least one writing assignment for nearly every reading. Many questions require students to synthesize information from other readings in the same chapter. Most of the questions, except where stated otherwise, are intended for individual responses. In addition, many of them can provide focus for classroom discussion or small-group work.

The Structure of the *Instructor's Notes*

The text of these notes is arranged to follow the main text chapter by chapter. For the rhetoric chapters (Chapters 1–21), the notes for each chapter outline some of the problems you might face while teaching it, suggest some solutions, and address the chapter exercises, with ideas for extending those exercises beyond the text. The exercises are open-ended, so our notes are, too: there are no easy answers to any of the problems we suggest in each chapter, and students can likely make good arguments for answers other than some of those that we have supplied. (Note that some exercises, especially those that might elicit especially varied or personal responses, are not addressed in these notes.)

For each of the chapters of readings, the corresponding chapter of the *Notes* begins with an introduction to the issues addressed in the chapter, along with some general questions that the issues raise. Then we provide possible answers for the Respond exercises at the end of each reading. Most questions in these exercises are open-ended, and the answers will vary; in many cases we've suggested one or more possibilities. No attempt has been made to provide answers for writing assignments. At the end of each chapter there are wrap-up exercises that incorporate material from two or more readings; some of these questions would be suitable for in-class essay writing.

We also provide a suggested classroom exercise for each reading. The concept behind the classroom exercises is to give each reading a session's worth (about an hour) of class time, although you may be budgeting class time very differently. Except where otherwise noted, the exercises are discussion questions based on the reading. Some of the classroom exercises focus on the content of the reading, some require students to think about the worlds they know in terms of the arguments presented in the reading, and some ask students to analyze the reading in terms of specific rhetorical techniques or lines of argument. In most cases, students should have done the reading already and perhaps answered one or more of the questions that follow it. With some modification, however, many of the questions could work well as pre-reading exercises to get students thinking about a topic or to explore their preconceptions. If your class is small, everyone can participate in a single discussion. You may, however, wish to break the class into small groups to maximize the speaking opportunities for every student. Be sure to save some time at the end of the session for groups to summarize their discussion for the whole class (this is great practice in summarizing and constructing oral arguments).

If your class periods are sufficiently long, give groups ten or fifteen minutes to prepare a discussion, and select one group to present its arguments and ideas to the class (for five or ten minutes). As an additional reinforcement, the other students can analyze and discuss the rhetorical techniques used in the group's presentation. If you retain the same groups over several discussion sessions, each group could have a turn at presenting its arguments to the entire class.

Instructor's Notes

Everything's an Argument with Readings

CHAPTER 1

Everything Is an Argument

The most important lesson in this chapter is that all language and even images can serve as argument. Some first-year students have difficulty understanding *argument* as anything but "disagreement" or "fight," and getting them to accept the word as meaning "making a point" or "reasoned inquiry" can prove challenging. A second important lesson in this chapter is that rhetorical situations vary widely, ranging from the obviously persuasive (Charles Murray's argument that only a small percentage of the population should go to college) to the poetic (Michael Lassell's poem about a brother's death). Understanding how arguments change depending on contexts and, in fact, understanding the contexts themselves can be challenging for students. Fortunately, even seemingly homogeneous classes usually are composed of students who carry different assumptions and who have varied cultural backgrounds and experiences. Have students practice analyzing arguments in class, and they'll probably encounter a broad range of knowledge, assumptions, and interpretations. Further, almost any student will be able to understand the concept of kairos (p. 27) and the idea that there are particular times when arguments will be more effective; most kids figured out this idea in negotiating with their parents years ago.

Stasis theory and the rhetorical appeals of ethos, pathos, and logos are powerful tools for understanding and creating arguments, but it may take students some time to sort them out. Students often rightly perceive the difficulty of separating the three appeals and treating them as distinct entities. In almost all rhetorical situations, the three appeals overlap significantly, so that, for example, an effective logical or emotional appeal builds a particular kind of ethos. They will also quickly realize that it can be difficult to find pure examples of the kinds of arguments that stasis theory introduces, but with work they should be able to see that many authors move through one or more stasis questions in making their arguments.

Stasis theory is a way of approaching an issue to find out where the points of agreement and disagreement lie. From its origins in Greek thought, stasis theory has described how to approach legal cases, and stasis theory is still, essentially, how lawyers brief a case. To help students understand stasis theory, you might consider walking through an imaginary crime in class. If someone goes missing, for example, there is a question of fact. Did something happen to this person? If a dead body is found, then investigators know that something happened and try to define the event: was it suicide, an accident, or a murder? If they can define the crime as murder, they might next evaluate it: was it murder in the first, second, or third degree? Cause becomes very important at the stasis of evaluation. When they have evaluated the severity of the crime, the judicial system makes a proposal about what to do next: should the criminal be given a prison sentence of a limited number of years, life imprisonment, or the death penalty?

Respond

From page 6 (top):
Can an argument really be any text that expresses a point of view? What kinds of arguments—if any—might be made by the following items?

- a Boston Red Sox cap **[The cap can assert a fan's support for a baseball team and affirm a sense of identity with other fans, a city, or even a region of the country. It could also be a taunt to fans of other teams, particularly the New York Yankees. It might also support the loyal tradition of Red Sox fans or celebrate their recent World Series wins.]**
- a Livestrong bracelet **[The bracelet may argue that the wearer is committed to cancer-research charities or to fashionable trends.]**
- the "explicit lyrics" label on a best-selling rock CD **[A label affixed to the CD might warn that the lyrics and themes in the album are unsuitable for children. Some people might avoid the CD for that reason, and others might select it because of the adult content.]**
- the health warning on a package of cigarettes **[The warning describes potential consequences of smoking; some**

consumers might decide not to buy the cigarettes as a result, and some might feel guilty about their purchase. This warning might also serve as a good example of a strong argument that nonetheless frequently fails to persuade.]

- a belated birthday card [**Such a card, often humorous, is frequently a plea for forgiveness or understanding, arguing that the sender deserves credit for remembering the birthday at all.**]
- a Rolex watch [**The watch might imply that the owner is wealthy and tasteful enough to select a much-admired, highly refined product, or it might argue that the owner wants to display his or her wealth as a mark of personal distinction.**]

From page 6 (bottom):

What are your reasons for making arguments? Keep notes for two days about every single argument you make, using our broad definition to guide you. Then identify your reasons: How many times did you aim to persuade? To convince? To inform or explain? To explore? To decide? To meditate?

- **This exercise will get your students writing early and require them to think seriously about their active participation in building arguments every day and about the very different contexts and goals of different arguments. You might remind them that text messages, posts to Facebook or other social media, or discussions about sports or music all count. It's likely that many of them will give up trying to catalog every argument they make over two days because there are just so many; their exhaustion with the exercise can serve as an argument in favor of the idea that everything's an argument.**

From page 17:

- **This exercise asks students to practice categorizing arguments and gets them to think critically about what contexts determine an argument's success. You might ask them to work in pairs or small groups on this exercise; the presence of other students will keep them more alert to the idea that an argument's success can depend in large part on the audience.**

From page 28:

What common experiences—if any—do the following objects, brand names, and symbols evoke, and for what audiences in particular? What sorts of appeals do they make: to pathos, ethos, or logos?

- a USDA organic label **[associated with healthy, environmentally friendly, and perhaps fresher-tasting food; for health-conscious consumers]**
- the golden arches **[associated with fast and relatively inexpensive food, convenience, efficiency, commercialism, American cultural imperialism, obesity; for children and families, perhaps travelers]**
- the Sean John label as seen on its Web site **[associated with urban style and hip-hop culture; for young, fashion-conscious consumers, particularly African Americans]**
- a can of Coca-Cola **[associated with refreshment, relaxation, tradition, the necessity of caffeine, holidays, or U.S. power and cultural hegemony; for a worldwide audience]**
- Sleeping Beauty's castle on the Disney logo **[associated with childhood stories, wonder, magic, entertainment, Florida vacations, corporate power; for children and families, with an especially nostalgic appeal to adults]**
- Oprah Winfrey **[associated with sensitivity, self-empowerment, success, generosity, perhaps emotional manipulation; particularly successful with female audiences but with a broad American appeal]**
- the Vietnam Veterans Memorial **[associated with a divisive war, the honor accorded those killed in the war, and attempts to help heal the divisions created by the war; for those close to soldiers who died and for the country at large]**
- Ground Zero at the World Trade Center site **[associated with tragedy, loss, heroism, resilience; for those who lost a loved one on 9/11 and for the country at large]**
- an AIDS ribbon **[associated with compassion, consciousness raising, activism, solidarity with those who have HIV/AIDS, and, especially during certain periods such as the mid-1990s, a particular kind of political correctness; for those who know someone with HIV/AIDS and those concerned about the spread of the disease and how it is treated]**

From page 29:
Take a look at the bumper sticker below, and then analyze it. What is its purpose? What kind of argument is it? Which of the stasis questions does it most appropriately respond to? To what audiences does it appeal? What appeals does it make and how? **[This bumper sticker makes an appeal to values by asking us to think carefully about how we define patriotism and how the choice of what we drive has larger effects. Encourage your students to think about the ethos of a person who might put this bumper sticker on a car and the ways that images and words make its argument.]**

CHAPTER 2

Arguments Based on Emotion: Pathos

If argument is primarily a form of reasoned inquiry, an idea suggested in Chapter 1, what is the role of emotion in a responsible argument? Students will certainly struggle, as we all do, with distinguishing between appropriate and inappropriate emotion since that distinction is determined by the rhetorical situation, especially the audience. Determining appropriate and inappropriate emotion requires judgment, and agreement is never guaranteed.

Students may also struggle with distinguishing between reason and emotion. This chapter includes excerpts from emotionally grounded arguments that are effective *because* they exist on the shifting border between emotion and reason (think of how Georgina Kleege uses the fact of her blindness to make an emotional appeal on pages 34 and 35). You might help your students see the relationships among reason, emotion, argument, and persuasion by drawing on the board a diagram that shows rational argument as a subset of persuasion. Such a diagram leaves room for emotional appeals as a legitimate part of argument and inquiry, an idea that some students resist. Before you show the diagram, though, you might have your students develop their own diagrams to illustrate the relationships. You might encourage students in discussion to brainstorm about emotional appeals that they feel are appropriate; we've found that appeals to patriotism, for example, can be powerfully persuasive for some students who thought they valued only facts and reason.

Respond

From page 33:
Working with a classmate, make a list of reasons why speakers in situations like this one (the President speaking on the death of

Osama bin Laden) would need to use emotional appeals cautiously, even sparingly. What consequences might heightened emotional appeals lead to? What is at stake for the speaker in such situations, in terms of credibility and ethos? **[Among other possible answers, students might note that President Obama does not want to incite anger that could possibly spread beyond strong feelings toward Osama bin Laden to anger toward Muslims generally. President Obama does not want to give bin Laden too much credit, and celebrating bin Laden's death too much would make bin Laden seem more powerful. President Obama wants to have a calm, authoritative ethos as president of the most powerful country in the world, so not going overboard on emotional appeals helps him maintain his authority. Also, President Obama does not want to seem to be celebrating the death of *anyone,* even a hated enemy, so much that he looks cold and heartless.]**

From pages 40–41:

1. To what specific emotions do the following slogans, sales pitches, and maxims appeal?
   - "Just do it." (ad for Nike) **[appeal to pleasure, boldness]**
   - "Think different." (ad for Apple computers) **[appeal to pride, creativity]**
   - "Reach out and touch someone." (ad for AT&T) **[appeal to love, joy, and pleasure]**
   - "Yes we can!" (2008 presidential campaign slogan for Barack Obama) **[appeal to hope, optimism, and community]**
   - "Country first." (2008 presidential campaign slogan for John McCain) **[appeal to patriotism and duty]**
   - "By any means necessary." (rallying cry from Malcolm X) **[appeal to fear or anxiety]**
   - "Have it your way." (slogan for Burger King) **[appeal to freedom, pleasure]**
   - "You can trust your car to the man who wears the star." (slogan for Texaco) **[appeal to anxiety, attachment, and security]**
   - "It's everywhere you want to be." (slogan for Visa) **[appeal to pleasure, anxiety, or security]**
   - "Know what comes between me and my Calvins? Nothing!" (tag line for Calvin Klein jeans) **[appeal to pleasure, sexual suggestion]**

- "Don't mess with Texas!" (antilitter campaign slogan) **[appeal to fear and empathy]**
- "Because You're Worth It" (ad for L'Oreal) **[appeal to pleasure, feelings of self-esteem, and luxury]**

2. **Most students can readily appreciate the connections between rhetoric and advertising, so asking them to determine how advertising uses rhetorical strategies can be an especially productive exercise. You might emphasize how different advertisers focus on different emotions. A magazine like *Spin*, aimed at a younger demographic than *Time*, is more likely to contain humorous advertisements. Ads in *Time* and *Newsweek* might appeal to the emotions that parents feel about their children since those magazines have an older audience.**

3–4. **These exercises ask students to think about arguments based on emotion in contexts that they might be more familiar with. For example, many students have probably noticed the difficulty of conveying tone and emotion in email and text messages, so they use emoticons and other signals (e.g., an abbreviation such as LOL) to signal emotional claims to their audiences. Humor in argument can make for good presentations and encourages students to think critically about texts that they encounter every day.**

 If you'd like to examine the use of emotional arguments over a longer period of time, you might ask students to do some research. Ask them to find texts of powerful speeches, such as Pericles's Funeral Oration, Martin Luther King Jr.'s "I Have a Dream," or Ronald Reagan's State of the Union addresses. Ask students to identify the emotional appeals *and* the logical appeals and to explain their combined effectiveness.

CHAPTER 3

Arguments Based on Character: Ethos

Aristotle says in the *Rhetoric* that the most important of the three proofs (logical, pathetic, ethical) is the argument based on character: if the audience does not trust the orator, all else is in vain. This chapter presents two primary difficulties for students. First, many students feel uncomfortable with the idea that ethos is context specific. They do not like the idea that good and honorable people can seek to change their self-presentation for different audiences without lying or misrepresenting themselves. Further, the idea that, say, Kim Kardashian has a more credible ethos than a senator or governor in the right context—for example, a cosmetics advertisement—bothers some students. But once they grasp the idea that context determines an argument's success, this idea that ethos can be elastic makes more sense.

The second and more important difficulty is that some first-year students find it a challenge to take on a voice they are not accustomed to and call it their own. Many students simply do not have the writing experience to believe that they have more than one voice or that they could develop a variety of voices for different rhetorical contexts. One of the great gifts that a writing class can give students, therefore, is confidence in their own authority.

Some students will want to argue that adopting different voices is a form of lying—by creating characters that do not exist or by taking on authority that is not theirs to claim. Explain to students that the written voices they use in class, in emails to family members, and in job applications, for example, already differ, but that they are not necessarily false representations. Instead, each of these three kinds of writing attempts to create a character that foregrounds certain elements of students' interests and expertise and backgrounds others.

Respond

1. Consider the ethos of these public figures. Then describe one or two products that might benefit from their endorsements as well as several that would not. **[Answers will vary; some suggestions are provided.]**

   - Cat Deeley—emcee of *So You Think You Can Dance* **[The model and television host likes to emphasize her quirkiness, but a big part of her appeal stems from what many perceive as effortless elegance; she has been extremely successful as a spokesperson for shampoo and other products related to beauty and fashion. She is especially popular in the United Kingdom.]**

   - Margaret Cho—comedian **[The outspoken comedian may offend many audiences, especially conservative audiences, with her politically charged humor. Her sympathy with gay, lesbian, bisexual, and transgender issues and her directness in talking about racial stereotypes and her own Asian American background have made her extremely popular in some minority communities.]**

   - Johnny Depp—actor **[The popular actor has had numerous images in his career—bad-boy sex symbol, political protestor, serious artist. Traditional product endorsements might mark Depp as a sellout, but he is probably serious enough to be involved with political causes; might have a broad appeal to the young as well as those in middle age.]**

   - Lady Gaga—singer and songwriter **[A provocative performer who often embraces the outrageous, Lady Gaga has been heavily involved with humanitarian causes and with feminist and lesbian, gay, bisexual, and transgender activism. She would probably appeal far more to younger audiences than she would older or more traditional audiences.]**

   - Bill O'Reilly—TV news commentator **[The aggressive, opinionated talk-show host works for the Fox News Channel; he usually advocates conservative causes with appeals to a blue-collar background and populist ethos; he probably should not endorse luxury goods or products that might seem frivolous.]**

- Marge Simpson—sensible wife and mother on *The Simpsons* **[The generally responsible cartoon housewife occasionally goes off the deep end and often appears naïve; she could be an advocate for any number of mainstream products but is not likely to represent upscale or serious (e.g., life insurance) products.]**
- Jon Stewart—host of *The Daily Show* on Comedy Central **[Extremely popular with young, liberal, and progressive audiences, Stewart occupies an odd space—some audiences would take him seriously as a straightforward voice of reason while others would dismiss him as fundamentally unserious because he hosts a fake news show.]**

2–3. You might use these exercises to emphasize how different audiences and different contexts lead to different strategies for building credibility and enhancing ethos. Exercise 2 would be especially good for challenging students to think of situations where public figures they do not like could still be authoritative. Exercise 3 is likely to be fascinating for students; you might have them work in pairs or groups to see if their own analysis of their ethos matches that of others.

You can extend the exercises in this chapter by asking students to list the many voices they have and the situations in which they are appropriate. Ask students to find things they have written for different audiences, or assign them a topic and a set of audiences. For example, have them write three emails announcing that they've been dismissed from school. How is it different to write this news to one's parents, one's best friend, one's high school teachers, or one's siblings? (Note that this assignment asks most students to assume a voice they can't imagine actually needing to assume.) Once they've written their samples, ask the students to find and annotate the textual cues that demonstrate shifting rhetorical ethos.

CHAPTER 4

Arguments Based on Facts and Reason: Logos

Finally, the good stuff: evidence, facts, testimony, statistics—real numbers, real facts, and no more opinions and feelings. That's the attitude some student writers will take. Students who feel lost without "solid facts" to support arguments will be happy to come to this chapter. But using evidence responsibly is complicated. Students will need to become comfortable critiquing facts as well as opinions, questioning surveys and statistical evidence, and uncovering assumptions that lie behind enthymemes. For example, you might introduce the factual claim that the Bayer company used to use in its aspirin advertising: "Nothing works better than Bayer." It's a fact: no aspirin works better than Bayer aspirin. But it's a fact that conceals the important point that other aspirins work equally well.

The concept of the arguable proposition might help students see that making a distinction between fact and opinion can sometimes be difficult. Certain propositions are not arguable: the square root of 100 is 10; Canada borders the United States; Jane Austen wrote in English. We do not argue about these claims because we accept them as commonplaces: they are, for most purposes, facts. But other facts are arguable: Christopher Columbus discovered America, William Shakespeare wrote all the plays attributed to him, clear-cutting in the rain forest has little environmental impact. At some point in the not-too-distant past, these last three facts were commonplaces, at least to certain audiences. But now they are arguable propositions: reasonable people could dispute the claims and offer other evidence in support of counterarguments.

Further, how we interpret statistics, or how we argue we should respond to statistics, can remind us that numbers and facts are rarely whole arguments in themselves. Instead, numbers are usually data points that we can use in particular rhetorical situations at particular times.

Respond

From page 60:

Discuss whether the following statements are examples of hard evidence **[inartistic]** or constructed arguments **[artistic]**. Not all cases are clear-cut.

1. Drunk drivers are involved in more than 50 percent of traffic deaths. **[inartistic; ask students to discuss how the word "involved" works in this claim.]**
2. DNA tests of skin found under the victim's fingernails suggest that the defendant was responsible for the assault. **[inartistic]**
3. A psychologist testified that teenage violence could not be blamed on video games. **[inartistic]**
4. An apple a day keeps the doctor away. **[artistic]**
5. The only thing we have to fear is fear itself. **[artistic]**
6. Air bags ought to be removed from vehicles because they can kill young children and small-framed adults. **[inartistic]**

From pages 63, 66, and 67:

This chapter distinguishes between artistic and inartistic proofs: the first relies on authorial invention (enthymemes, syllogisms, analogies, and so on), and the second on specific pieces of evidence. Our experience has been that first-year writers are drawn to the inartistic appeals out of a belief that nothing convinces like hard evidence—the "facts" that seem inarguable. You will need to help your students see the effectiveness of artistic appeals, too. We offer several excerpts that you could use to explore artistic appeals, but a quick look at any newspaper op-ed page will reveal many more examples. As an introduction to Toulmin logic and as evidence for the idea that artistic appeals can be effective, have your students find the claims and reasons embedded in newspaper editorials. Student newspapers also offer, in our experience, examples of *ineffective* artistic appeals. First-year writers are usually able to explain what has gone wrong in an unpersuasive opinion piece, and you could profitably steer class discussion to the author's use of evidence.

CHAPTER 5

Fallacies of Argument

Our experience has been that first-year writers can really enjoy a unit on fallacies. They particularly enjoy finding the fallacies in writing by those with whom they disagree. Sometimes, though, they can even enjoy spotting fallacies in their own papers—it's a little embarrassing to have fallacious reasoning pointed out, but students usually appreciate the help.

Fallacies are not always mortal errors in argument. They represent reasoning that is in *some way* faulty or that is likely to be rejected by a *particular* audience. Arguments that one audience might accept another audience might reject because they consider the reasoning fallacious. Perhaps no fallacy illustrates this problem better than the idea of the overly sentimental appeal (see p. 77). If you or someone you love has been a victim of gun violence, you might find heartwrenching emotional appeals to be entirely appropriate. If you or someone you love has successfully used a gun in self-defense, you might make a strongly emotional appeal on the other side of the issue. Or consider the *ad hominem* fallacy. In some cases, what some consider a tough challenge of someone's ethos might look to others like an *ad hominem* attack. Our point is that one person's fallacy can sometimes be another person's successful argument. Fallacies are not always clear cases.

The fallacies listed in this chapter constitute only a few of the many that logicians and rhetoricians have identified through the years. If you have time and interest, you could ask your students to do research into the topic of fallacies and have them present other fallacies that they find. If you combine this chapter with the one on evidence, you could also make this a disciplines-based activity since fallacies differ from field to field. Another possible classroom activity might be to have students see how many fallacies they can squeeze into one piece of writing, and how much they can exaggerate these fallacies.

Respond

1. Examine each of the following political slogans or phrases for logical fallacies.

   - "Resistance is futile." (Borg message on *Star Trek*) **[Scare tactic, begging the question, possibly dogmatism]**
   - "It's the economy, stupid." (sign on the wall at Bill Clinton's campaign headquarters) **[bandwagon appeal; possibly faulty causality]**
   - "Remember the Alamo." (battle cry) **[possibly a *non sequitur* or faulty causality]**
   - "Make love, not war." (antiwar slogan popularized during the Vietnam War) **[either/or; dogmatism]**
   - "A chicken in every pot." (campaign slogan) **[possibly a *non sequitur* or faulty causality]**
   - "Guns don't kill, people do." (NRA slogan) **[faulty causality]**
   - "If you can't stand the heat, get out of the kitchen." (attributed to Harry S. Truman) **[either/or]**
   - "Yes we can!" (Obama campaign slogan) **[bandwagon appeal; possibly dogmatism]**

2–4. Exercises 2 and 3 ask students to find fallacies in other texts. These exercises might prove to be difficult, but that difficulty will help students understand that many so-called fallacies are audience-specific. Exercise 4, which asks students to see how other writers read fallacies, might also reinforce the slipperiness of calling an argument fallacious.

CHAPTER 6

Rhetorical Analysis

This chapter puts together many principles from earlier chapters and asks students to use those principles as analytical tools. (The next few chapters emphasize how rhetoric can help them produce arguments.) The rhetorical concepts that the book has introduced help students to understand how and why people make the arguments that they do. First-year writers, who bring a range of experiences and abilities to the classroom, may know some of these concepts under different names. "Making a claim," for example, could be the equivalent of "writing a thesis." "Giving an argument shape" might be understood as "organizing." Students probably also can make sense of the differences between claims of emotion, character, and fact: they see such claims every day, and learning to think rhetorically can be understood as a way of organizing and commenting on ideas that they intuitively grasp. Once they can articulate these ideas, they can think, read, and write more consciously and critically.

Encourage your students to explore their familiarity with these concepts by asking them to name examples of each of the categories of argument. Popular advertisements are a good tool for showing students the power of carefully crafted appeals; students have sometimes studied advertisements in psychology classes, and they come to think of advertising as a series of tricks. But rhetorical analysis can help them see advertising—and therefore many other forms of discourse—as communication that they can understand. And what they can understand in others' arguments they can apply to their own.

As we mention below in the Respond section, if you have students work on rhetorical analysis, whether it's a major writing assignment or in-class group work, make sure that they choose clearly argumentative texts to analyze. We've had many students try to write rhetorical analyses of news stories, and it usually ends in frustration; to analyze the rhetoric of a news article usually just requires too much sophistication, and producing a strong rhetorical analysis paper is difficult enough because the rhetorical appeals are so intertwined in most arguments. If your students are choosing their own arguments to write about, steer them toward pieces that are clearly marked as opinion. And if you do assign a rhetorical analysis, we recommend modeling the process for students in class and calling their attention to the excellent sample essay in the textbook (pp. 111–13).

Respond

From page 95:
Describe a persuasive moment that you can recall from a speech, an editorial, an advertisement, a YouTube clip, or a blog posting. Or research one of the following famous persuasive moments and describe the circumstances—the historical situation, the issues at stake, the purpose of the argument—that make it so memorable.

- Abraham Lincoln's "Gettysburg Address" (1863) **[the turning point of the American Civil War, a reaffirmation of core Union values]**
- Elizabeth Cady Stanton's "Declaration of Sentiments" at the Seneca Falls Convention (1848) **[a key statement of principles and arguments for women's rights]**
- Chief Tecumseh's address to General William Henry Harrison (1810) **[an argument for the unity of Native American tribes against American settlers based on a history of betrayal of American Indians by white settlers]**
- Winston Churchill's addresses to the British people during World War II (1940) **[an attempt to rally a nation against a Nazi military onslaught threatening Britain]**
- Martin Luther King Jr.'s "Letter from Birmingham Jail" (1963) **[an attempt to remind white Christian leaders of the religious roots of the civil rights movement and to defend the principles of nonviolent civil disobedience]**
- Ronald Reagan's tribute to the *Challenger* astronauts (1986) **[a eulogy for the astronauts killed in the explosion of the space shuttle and an argument for continuing space exploration]**
- Toni Morrison's speech accepting the Nobel Prize (1993) **[an assertion of a feminist, African American presence in literature and theory by the first African American woman to win a Nobel Prize in Literature]**
- will.i.am and The Black Eyed Peas' "Yes We Can" song/collage on YouTube (2008) **[an argument early in the Democratic**

**primaries that quotes Obama's New Hampshire conces-
sion speech; an argument that Barak Obama is an inspiring leader who can bring together diverse voices
and people]**

From pages 100 and 107:

These exercises ask a great deal of students and could easily serve
as paper assignments. One of the most difficult aspects of a rhetorical analysis is that after students work hard to pull apart the different
aspects of an argument, they're asked to put them all back together
to make a judgment on the argument's overall effectiveness. As we
say above, make sure that your students choose clearly argumentative texts to analyze. Though it's certainly possible to present an
excellent rhetorical analysis of a news article, that may be a more
challenging assignment than most first-year writing students should
take on for their first rhetorical analysis. You might consider taking
any one of these exercises and modeling the response for your class
to help build their confidence before they begin their own rhetorical
analyses.

CHAPTER 7

Structuring Arguments

We all need help structuring arguments, so be ready to spend some time on this chapter. Even many of the strongest first-year writers have only one model, the five-paragraph essay, for organizing their writing. Too often, that model is overly rigid for them; they focus on counting paragraphs rather than using the format as a way of shaping an argument. The classical oration will not be a big leap for those who know the five-paragraph model, and it might help some students realize that the important concept for organizing their essays is working through the logic of the claim, not just filling in the required number of sentences and paragraphs.

Rogerian argument and Toulmin logic will likely prove more difficult for students to master. With Rogerian rhetoric, the key idea will be the importance of taking opposing positions seriously and treating them fairly. For many students, political arguments, particularly the zero-sum arguments of political elections, provide the primary model for thinking about argument and persuasion. But in academic argument, which is the writing that most students will be doing in the next few years, the goal of an argument might be better understood as entering a conversation and modifying or refining other positions, not defeating the competition and scoring a win.

Toulmin logic can seem complicated at first—so many concepts, so many terms. But for reasons that we explain in the chapter, Toulmin logic can also be powerful as an analytic and productive tool. Our experience has been that when first-year students commit themselves to understanding and using the Toulmin framework, their writing improves noticeably. Students begin to make arguments that use evidence effectively, and they write papers that show greater sensitivity to audience. The system holds students accountable for every part of their argument, while forcing them to question the foundations and assumptions underlying their claims.

But like any complicated system, Toulmin logic takes time to learn. Do not expect your students to become comfortable with the concepts immediately. Instead, plan to introduce and review the various elements of Toulmin argument over a period of weeks. Take your time leading students through the idea of claims and reasons. These two key elements might take a week to explain completely, especially if you use real-world examples in which claims and reasons are not made explicit. (Letters to the editor of any newspaper will illustrate the problems of making clear claims supported by coherent reasons. Some letters will serve as examples of good, clear writing; others will make great counterexamples.)

Students usually struggle with the idea that there are two kinds of evidence—in support of reasons and of warrants—and that an argument might be exemplary in its use of one while completely ignoring the other. The Toulmin system gives you a way of explaining to your students exactly what the evidentiary problems are in their arguments. You can praise a student's use of statistical evidence in support of the reasons, for instance, while asking him or her to provide more evidence in support of the warrant. Our experience has been that when students come to understand the distinction between these two forms of evidence, they also learn to create more effective enthymemes: students can work backward from evidence to claims.

Respond

From page 131:
You might use this exercise to reinforce the idea of the importance of argument structure. For example, if a student chooses a controversial issue such as abortion, Rogerian argument would probably not be a good choice for an audience of true believers on either side of the issue.

From pages 133, 140, and 145:
You can help students learn Toulmin logic by taking every opportunity to use the terminology in class. The more students hear the words, the more comfortable they will be using them themselves. (We have gone so far sometimes as to state *everything* in class as claim, reasons, and warrant: "Claim: Rob, you should help me arrange the desks in a circle. Reason: Because I want everyone to see each other in the discussion. Warrant: Seeing other students in a discussion is good. Warrant: If I want a student to do something in class, the student should do it." Or if a student says she is hungry, we restate it: "Claim: I am hungry. Reason: Because I have not eaten

since last night.") Some students might complain about the complicated system. Help these students make their complaints using Toulmin logic: "Claim: I do not like learning Toulmin logic. Reason: Toulmin is too complicated." You can examine these claims, explore the reasons and warrants, and show your students why Toulmin will help them. In short, use the system to show how powerful it can be.

A final note: students work hard in other classes to learn complicated systems. Every academic field has terminology and a taxonomy that take time to learn. You should make no apologies for teaching difficult material. Toulmin is hard to learn, but the effort is repaid many times over. (Enthymeme: If students work hard to learn in any other classes, then they can expect to work hard to learn in a writing class, too.)

CHAPTER 8

Arguments of Fact

This is the first chapter that deals explicitly with the stases that were introduced in Chapter 1. The first stasis question in the ancients' tradition was of fact: did something happen? Before an argument can progress to the next stage, everyone must agree that something did happen. Consider a missing-person case. If no one knows where the person is and no body can be found, then authorities cannot arrest and try someone for murder, decide that an accident occurred, or rule the death a suicide. First, there must be agreement that something happened; only after the parties have agreed that *something* has happened can they determine which term or definition best applies. An argument of fact is the basis of further claims.

Your students may find arguments of fact to be especially interesting because they have long understood facts to be immutable. Problems arise, however, when they begin to consider what kinds of facts can be reasonably argued and what kinds cannot be reasonably argued. There's no easy answer to this question. For instance, consider the statement that there has been only one Roman Catholic president of the first forty-four; such a claim hardly seems arguable. A quick look in any encyclopedia would confirm this fact. But what if a historian found evidence that an earlier president was a Roman Catholic who had suppressed his religious affiliation because he feared the anti-Catholic prejudice that was common in the late nineteenth century? In that case, even this seemingly straightforward, easily verified claim becomes arguable. A good argument with good evidence can make new facts.

This example, which falls far afield from the work that students will produce in their classes, nonetheless might help them understand that facts can be arguable. They may, however, find it difficult to come up with topics of their own that are manageable in the papers they'll be writing for class. Research will play a crucial role in developing good factual arguments, and the brainstorming exercises included below should help them sort out which arguments would be particularly viable for a paper.

Respond

From page 155:
For each topic in the following list, decide whether the claim is worth arguing to a college audience, and explain why or why not. **[Answers will vary; some suggestions are provided, though for most of the "worth arguing" answers the same idea applies: the claims need evidence to be accepted.]**

- Hurricanes are increasing in number and ferocity. **[Worth arguing; how far back does reliable data reach? How well could we measure hurricane strength before the Saffir-Simpson scale was created? How do we compare hurricanes that are now hitting populated coastal areas to those that hit coastal areas with few residents?]**
- Many people die annually of heart disease. **[Not worth arguing; the claim can be easily supported by one or two numbers.]**
- Fewer people would die of colon and prostate cancer each year if they drank more coffee. **[worth arguing]**
- Japan might have come to terms more readily in 1945 if the Allies in World War II hadn't demanded unconditional surrender. **[worth arguing]**
- Boys would do better in school if there were more men teaching in elementary and secondary classrooms. **[worth arguing]**
- The ongoing economic recession will lead drivers to buy more energy-efficient vehicles. **[Worth arguing; for one thing, the recession might lead people *not* to buy cars.]**
- There aren't enough high-paying jobs for college graduates these days. **[Worth arguing; what constitutes enough? What do we consider high pay?]**
- Hydrogen may never be a viable alternative to fossil fuels because it takes too much energy to change hydrogen into a useable form. **[Worth arguing; how much energy is too much? What if we run out of fossil fuels or if obtaining them becomes too costly?]**
- Its opponents have grossly exaggerated the costs of the Patient Protection and Affordable Care Act of 2010. **[worth**

arguing; even if everyone agrees on the costs, which is unlikely, there might still be debate over whether there was gross exaggeration]

From pages 158 and 160:

These exercises would be especially useful for helping students brainstorm paper topics of their own. First-year writing students often find that it's difficult to come up with reasonable factual claims for short papers. You might use the exercise from page 158 as group work in class. Immediate peer review of topic ideas will help some students see how reasonable their claims might be as well as how much work individual claims might require. The exercise from page 160 gives students a number of examples of factual arguments to look at as models. You might also direct them to www.snopes.com, a site that examines urban legends, for enjoyable examples of factual arguments.

Projects

As we mention above, perhaps the greatest difficulty in writing a factual argument is finding a topic that makes sense for a paper, so these projects can be a great starting point. If you allow students to choose their own topics, you might devote some class time to reading each of these projects aloud and having students talk through their ideas. Students can sometimes be overly protective of their ideas, afraid that someone else will steal precious jewels from them, but we've had great success having students talk through their ideas early in the writing process. They will often hear someone else introduce an idea that sparks their own imagination, or they'll qualify, counter, or modify an argument that someone else introduces. We have found that many students panic when they first receive an assignment and that even five or ten minutes spent in class exploring possible options can alleviate their anxiety and put them on the path toward selecting a workable topic. Be sure to build in a topic proposal stage for any of these projects that you assign; that will allow you to catch problem topics early so that students can find a better option.

CHAPTER 9

Arguments of Definition

A traditional legal example of stasis theory's practical application concerns a missing urn. This example works well in the classroom as an introduction to arguments of definition: an urn is discovered to be missing from a house and is found in the house of another person. At the level of fact, there is agreement: the defendant has the urn that belongs to the plaintiff. But there is considerable disagreement about definition: the plaintiff argues that the urn was stolen, whereas the defendant argues that it was merely *borrowed*. The case can go no further until the parties settle the question of definition. Only after the parties have defined "theft" and "borrowing" and only after they have determined which term best applies can the case move forward.

Toulmin logic will help you explain the contested, rhetorical nature of definitional claims. Because definitional criteria are warrants, they must be chosen with the audience in mind (if the audience members do not accept the criteria you choose, they will not accept any other part of the argument). You could return to the urn example to demonstrate the need for *shared* definitions of theft or borrowing. If, for example, you were to argue that borrowing without explicit permission constitutes theft, you would need to provide evidence for that criterion; your evidence must be tailored to a particular audience. Not everyone would accept that criterion: what about close friends or siblings who share their possessions without needing permission each time they borrow something?

Some students who struggle will be able to place an object within a given class (a fiddle is certainly a violin; prostitution is an exploitative business; paid workers are not volunteers) but will balk at the need to explore or defend definitional criteria. Turn to Toulmin to show that they might have evidence in support of their reasons but not in support of the warrants—the definitional criteria themselves.

Respond

From page 190:
Briefly discuss how you might define the italicized terms in the following controversial claims of definition. Compare your definitions of the terms with those of your classmates. **[Answers will vary; some possibilities are offered.]**

- Graphic novels are *serious literature.* **[must offer some psychological depth and some meaning beyond the surface; must be of high enough quality to be read for decades or centuries; must offer some kind of commentary on the human condition]**
- Burning a nation's flag is a *hate crime.* **[must be a crime or prosecutable act; must be aimed at a specific group; must be intended to hurt, demean, or disparage]**
- Matt Drudge and Arianna Huffington aren't *journalists.* **[must earn a living by reporting the news; must be trained in journalism either by schooling or through practical experience; must report the news ethically and responsibly]**
- College sports programs have become *big businesses.* **[must generate considerable income; must be enterprises that aim at constant growth; must be regional or national in scope; must make decisions to ensure their own success or profit]**
- Plagiarism can be an act of *civil disobedience.* **[must be a conscious act of lawbreaking; must be an act intended to question the legitimacy of the law being broken; must be a violation with legal consequences; must be an act for which the perpetrator is willing to accept the consequences]**
- Satanism is a *religion* properly protected by the First Amendment. **[must be a set of beliefs about the ultimate meaning or focus of life; must have beliefs that are shared by a group; must have beliefs that have a bearing on the conduct of one's life]**
- Campaign contributions are acts of *free speech* that should never be regulated. **[must be an expression of an idea through language, written or oral; must be an expression of a political character or with a political interest; must be noncommercial and nonthreatening]**

- The District of Columbia should not have all the privileges of an American *state*. **[must be a discrete territory in a relationship with the United States of America; must be a territory of reasonable size; must be a unit with economic and social diversity; must have historical significance as a territory]**
- Polygamous couples should have the legal privileges of *marriage*. **[must be an enduring bond between adults; must be a bond established to sustain family life; must be a sacramental bond; must be a sexual union]**

From page 192:

These exercises offer suggestions for helping students think of their own definitional claims by extending examples in the text. Another good exercise is for students to come up with far-fetched definitional claims: Oprah Winfrey is a cult leader; Disney is a virus; Tom Cruise is an alien. We've seen students write engaging, thoughtful arguments on these seemingly bizarre topics. Students often gravitate to topics such as capital punishment or abortion when writing definition arguments; however, when they approach the assignment more creatively, they seem to structure their arguments more effectively and develop their criteria in unexpected but reasonable ways. (An alien doesn't have to come from outer space, for example; maybe the world of celebrity that Tom Cruise inhabits is so different from ours that it may as well be an alien world.) When students write about the more creative claims and experiment with offbeat arguments, they have a greater opportunity to say something fresh.

Projects

The suggested projects can be extremely helpful for getting students thinking about their own topics; as we say above, definition arguments often work well if, as projects 2 and 3 advise, students get away from obvious topics and get creative with their approaches. If you have students who want to work on the fourth project, be sure to discuss with them that they need to allow sufficient time for questionnaires and surveys to be written, completed, and returned. We've seen many a project go off the rails because of a lack of planning for response times.

CHAPTER 10

Evaluations

In the notes for Chapter 9, we explained the classic illustration of the missing urn: the urn belonging to one person is found in the home of another. The parties disagree about the nature of the incident. One says the urn was stolen, and the other says it was merely borrowed. The matter is stuck at the level of definition, but let's imagine that the court decides the urn was stolen. The defendant might argue that he stole the urn for a good reason: the urn contained water that he needed for his ill child. The defendant now makes an argument of evaluation: the act of theft was, he claims, praiseworthy.

You can use the story of the urn to show your students how arguments of evaluation grow out of arguments of definition. The transition from definition to evaluation can be tricky, however; as you're writing, it's not always clear when you're defining and when you're evaluating. (For example, if you define someone as a hero, isn't that also an evaluation?) Nevertheless, most students will benefit from thinking of the two as separate, at least in the abstract.

Many students will need help choosing the level of evaluative abstraction for their arguments. It's one thing to argue that *Mission: Impossible* is great art; it's something else to argue that it's a good Tom Cruise blockbuster. The best argument probably lies between those extremes, and most students will need help crafting a strong, arguable thesis. Some students will be content to argue that something is good or bad; push them to complicate their ideas so that they write more interesting arguments.

As with arguments of definition, evaluative arguments challenge students to defend their criteria. Toulmin logic will show that criteria are warrants and must be developed with audience in mind. If the audience does not accept the criteria, the evaluative judgment will not be accepted either. Peer review or other forms of draft response will provide students with an audience of thoughtful readers who might challenge writers' criteria.

Respond

From pages 216, 221, and 223:
These exercises highlight the importance of developing evaluative criteria, which in our experience has been the step that most frustrates students. Because students generally feel comfortable with evaluative arguments in some form (such as for movies and sports), they can usually generate topics and claims with ease. They tend to have more difficulty tailoring criteria to specific audiences. With supplementary exercises, therefore, we recommend that you focus on helping them think about the warrants for particular claims, a skill that they can then transfer to their papers.

From page 218:
Choose one item from the following list that you understand well enough to evaluate. Develop several criteria of evaluation that you could defend to distinguish excellence from mediocrity in the area. Then choose an item that you don't know much about and explain the research you might do to discover reasonable criteria of evaluation for it.

- digital cameras
- NFL quarterbacks
- social networking sites
- TV journalists
- video games
- fashion designers
- Navajo rugs
- U.S. vice presidents
- organic vegetables
- hot water heaters
- spoken word poetry
- athletic shoes
- country music bands
- hip-hop bands

Answers will vary considerably. You might use this exercise as an in-class activity, having students work in groups ac-

cording to which topics they know best. **Many students will be surprised by how many criteria the group can come up with and how challenging it can be to establish criteria that many people can accept. When they research a topic that they don't know well, you might need to work with some students to push them beyond Wikipedia and the first three sites that come up in a Web search.**

From page 226:
Take a close look at the cover of Alison Bechdel's graphic novel *Fun Home: A Family Tragicomic.* In what various ways does it make an argument of evaluation designed to make you want to buy the book? Examine other books, magazines, or media packages (such as video game or software boxes) and describe any strategies they use to argue for their merit.

- **Students are likely to gravitate, rightly, to the top of the cover, where the phrase "National Bestseller" is printed in large capital letters and a quotation from *Time* magazine praises the book. You might push students to explain what they find appealing (or not) about the graphic design of the cover, too; in that discussion, the class is likely to discover that their classmates have different criteria about what constitutes an effective, inviting cover. You might also extend the exercise by asking students about fallacies (e.g., the bandwagon effect of "National Bestseller") that they find in the promotional materials that they talk about.**

Projects

We've found that students generally don't need a great deal of help developing evaluative claims. It can be more challenging to get students to write an *interesting* or *successful* evaluation; in particular, you'll probably need to encourage some students to be more explicit about their criteria and the warrants that support their criteria. Project 4 would be especially useful in helping students think through how to articulate criteria for evaluation; you might even use it as an in-class exercise to help demonstrate that the criteria for evaluation are arguments in themselves. Students have to defend the criteria if they want to defend their evaluative claims.

If you have students who find it difficult to make an evaluative *academic* argument, you might steer them toward project 2. Because the prompt emphasizes the idea of entering an ongoing conversation and staking one's claim by disagreeing with or qualifying the arguments of others, it sets students up for success in writing an academic argument.

CHAPTER 11

Causal Arguments

In some versions of the stases, causal arguments came before arguments of evaluation; in others, they came after. Show your class (by using the examples from this book or from elsewhere) that regardless of their place in the order of the stases, causal arguments build on and set up other arguments. Like definitions and evaluations, they rarely appear in pure form, though we provide some examples of such pure causal arguments in the text. The situations that open the chapter suggest such ideal causal arguments, though they also rely on definitional issues.

Causal arguments can be extremely challenging for students; the logic of causality is complex, the evidence is often shaky, and the results can be uncertain. We have found that students typically try to tackle causal arguments that reach too far for a regular class paper; it's too much to explain the effects of the French Revolution in four or five pages. Because the logic of causal arguments can be complex, students will likely benefit from extra time and help as they make causal claims. For useful models, you might turn to sports writing. Students can easily see how reasonable, informed observers can differ on why a team or an individual won or lost a competition.

Respond

From page 248:
The causes of some of the following events and phenomena are well-known and frequently discussed. But do you understand them well enough to spell out the causes to someone else? Working in a group, see how well (and in how much detail) you can explain each of the following events or phenomena. Which explanations are relatively clear, and which seem more open to debate?

- earthquakes/tsunamis **[clear]**
- popularity of Lady Gaga or *Jersey Shore* **[open to debate]**
- Cold War **[open to debate]**

- subprime mortgage crisis or GM bankruptcy **[open to debate]**
- AIDS pandemic in Africa **[open to debate]**
- popularity of the *Transformers* films **[open to debate]**
- swelling caused by a bee sting **[clear]**
- sharp rise in cases of autism or asthma **[open to debate]**
- climate change **[open to debate]**

From page 252:

This exercise is a great example of how a large-group exercise can help students develop a topic. Once your students have compiled a fairly long list, have them talk out how they might go about writing the argument. What research would they do? How would they qualify or limit the claim?

From page 254:

Answers will vary.

From page 256:

This exercise is a bit like our suggestion that students write unusual, or even eccentric, definition arguments. Oddball topics keep students' interest, but the real advantage to having students write them is that they learn a great deal about how to structure the argument. With a humorous or outlandish topic, students have to pay attention to form in a way that will benefit more serious writing assignments.

Projects

As we mention above, causal arguments can be difficult, and the projects here are designed to help students through different types of difficulty. If your students are working on a causal paper or project, encourage them to read through all of the projects, as they each highlight different ideas that students should consider in constructing their project. Project 1, for example, is fairly directive about offering students potential topics, which will allow them to place their energy into research. Project 2 nicely emphasizes the complexity of any, even seemingly simple, causal arguments by reminding students to tease out the differences between proximate causes and necessary causes. Project 4 releases students from the obligation to write an argument that nails down one cause-and-effect relationship and instead allows them the freedom to be more speculative.

CHAPTER 12

Proposals

This chapter provides students with the opportunity to put all their previous work in the service of a complex argument. Proposal arguments have been popular in our classes because most students see them as the culmination of the semester's effort: once students have learned to analyze and produce arguments of definition, evaluation, and causation, proposal arguments make more sense. You can ask students to define terms carefully, to explain their evaluative criteria, or to explore the causal connections more thoroughly. If you review the stases before you teach the proposal argument, students will understand that the proposal does not exist in a vacuum but instead builds on what's come before. Further, no other student-written argument seems to lend itself to a variety of student presentations as well as the proposal argument, so you might allow students more options for how they present their proposals—they can really tailor their presentation of the argument to a specific audience.

Some students enjoy writing about practical problems on campus or in the community, though in recent years we've found that many students think policy issues can make good papers, too, though you'll want to be careful that students don't tackle too much: sometimes they try to resolve world hunger in five pages. If your students write policy proposals, be sure to teach them the dangers of biting off more than they can chew. Requiring topic proposals, even short two- or three-sentence descriptions of what they want to work on, can make their arguments much more manageable.

We have asked students in our classes to do extensive audience analysis as part of the writing process. The chapter's guide to writing proposal arguments gives students some ideas about audience analysis, but you can go beyond what we provide. In the early stages of the writing process, ask students to write about their audience and consider the approaches that will be most rhetorically effective. Remind your students that if a proposal is to be accepted, it needs to be finely tuned to the demands of its audience. Sometimes you will have to work hard to push students beyond easy formulations of "average people" or "typical Americans" (often a code for "people who think like me") when they're defining their audiences.

Respond

From pages 275 and 279:
The exercises focus on two key issues for proposal arguments: developing claims that represent responses to real problems and tailoring proposals to a specific audience. Extend the exercises by asking students to examine a variety of proposals—from editorials in the student newspaper to large-scale governmental policy proposals—in terms of those same issues. How have the writers of policy proposals identified a real problem that's worth solving? How have editorial writers targeted their audience in their proposals? Also, consider asking students to identify the proposals that might be hidden within other forms of argument: is the writer making a proposal without seeming to?

Projects

Proposal projects are often the final assignment in a first-year writing class since they involve all of the stages. Proposals often seem to be the project about which students are the most earnest, too, which can be a benefit because they're especially interested in the issue. On the other hand, students who feel strongly about their proposal can sometimes be especially resistant to researching their topic. Projects 1 and 4 will be especially useful for helping you offer more thoughtful approaches for the student who has a good idea about a proposal but doesn't know how to go about completing the work. Project 2 offers students the opportunity to write about a topic that is probably close to their hearts. Project 3 will give students the chance to experiment with writing humor and might offer a fine way to cap a semester.

CHAPTER 13

Style in Arguments

Figurative language is so prevalent—we argue in the chapter that it is "indispensable to language use"—that students will be able to find and analyze examples of figures from almost any source. This chapter might best be approached as part of another unit so you can show the relationship between figures and definition, for example. Metaphor is a definitional argument, after all. By combining this chapter with others, you can illustrate the ways figures argue and are not merely dressing on top of already established arguments. You can also push students to think carefully about what tropes they can include in their own arguments. Too often, students do not think much about their style, in part because they don't have the means to understand how to write stylishly. But it doesn't take much exposure to different examples of stylish writing to develop a feel for how to improve one's own style.

Don't hesitate to draw connections between style in writing and style in dressing. Students who are alert to nuances of details in clothing can help the rest of the class understand the importance of details and presentation in writing. A student who understands that we dress for a variety of reasons—not just to cover ourselves and not just for comfort—might be a little closer to understanding that we don't just always "say what we mean." The best writers, like the best dressers, pay attention to the effects of small choices. Further, style is more than just ornamentation, as this chapter explains. Style, in writing or in clothing, helps create meaning.

Respond

From page 312:
Work with a classmate to revise Miller's paragraph, making sure that every sentence begins the same way, with the subject first. Then

read the passage aloud and see if it sounds much less effective and memorable. It's the variety in sentence openings that does the trick! **Answers may vary, but here's one way the paragraph might look:**

Happy Rogers, age eight, stands among her classmates in the schoolyard at dismissal time, immune, it seems to the cacophonous din. Hilton Augusta Parker Rogers, nicknamed Happy, is a poised and precocious blonde. She would be at home in the schoolyard of any affluent American suburb or big-city private school. But Happy is in the minority here at the elite, bilingual Nanyang Primary School in Singapore, her Dakota Fanning hair shimmering in a sea of darker heads. Her parents have traveled halfway around the world for this. Happy is navigating her friendships and doing her homework entirely in Mandarin while her American peers are feasting on the idiocies fed to them by junk TV and summer movies.

From pages 313, 315, and 323:

These exercises ask students to become more conscious of style both as readers and as writers. The productive exercises from pages 315 and 323 use learning tactics that are thousands of years old; students have been writing with schemes and tropes since at least the fifth century B.C. These kinds of exercises have persisted because they succeed—by helping students to recognize figurative language in others' sentences and to identify and use schemes and tropes more naturally in their own everyday writing.

You might challenge your students to find figures or tropes that we have not listed in this chapter. They could do research into the ancient rhetorical terms, perhaps starting with the Web site *Silvae Rhetoricae* (http://rhetoric.byu.edu/) or Ward Farnsworth's book *Farnsworth's Classical English Rhetoric*. Have them practice identifying and creating some of the figures that they find in these sources.

Or give students a piece of writing that is rich with figurative language and ask them to identify each of the figures. Are there any sentences that seem to contain no schemes or tropes? Could it be that these sentences are figurative in ways students don't expect or recognize? Remind them that figures represent changes in the ordinary syntax or signification; how might these remaining sentences be read as different from the ordinary?

From page 325:
Identify the figurative language used in the following slogans:

- "Energy drink with attitude." (Red Eye) **[personification, hyperbole]**
- "Open happiness." (Coca-Cola) **[irony ("open" has double meaning); metaphor]**
- "Melts in your mouth, not in your hands." (M&M's) **[parallelism]**
- "Be all that you can be." (U.S. Army) **[reversed structure]**
- "Breakfast of champions." (Wheaties) **[hyperbole, antonomasia]**
- "America runs on Dunkin'." (Dunkin' Donuts) **[hyperbole, metaphor]**
- "Got milk?" (America's Milk Processors) **[rhetorical question]**

CHAPTER 14

Visual and Multimedia Arguments

As we suggested in earlier notes, most students are familiar with some techniques of visual argument even if they are not able to analyze those techniques critically. Images occupy such a large part of students' daily lives—in advertisements, on television, even in textbooks—that they are almost bombarded by visual arguments. But your students may need a framework for understanding such arguments so that they can review them critically in what they read and use them honestly in what they write.

This chapter offers that framework and takes a highly rhetorical approach to visual arguments. That is, the chapter does more than make recommendations about choosing fonts or effectively positioning items on a page (though it includes such advice as well); it also asks students to ponder the rhetorical impact of visual texts and images on readers.

The final sections of the chapter offer advice on reading and writing visual texts, as well as focus on rhetorical concepts. For instance, the elements of successful visual presentations are arranged according to the three appeals discussed earlier in the book so that writers are asked to consider visual arguments based on ethos, pathos, and logos. You might ask students to offer more examples of how these appeals translate when operating in highly visual texts such as advertisements or magazine covers. Indeed, magazine advertising is a rich source of visual arguments because almost all ads make the same claim: the reader should buy our product.

Once your class is comfortable analyzing advertisements, you could move on to other visual arguments, such as textbook illustrations, statistical charts and graphs, product logos, and photojournalism—all of which are visually represented in this chapter.

Respond

From pages 328, 334, and 339:
These exercises encourage students to write about visual images, a challenging task. Help your students develop a rich vocabulary of visual arguments by pointing them to the questions in the chapter under the heading "Analyzing Visual Elements of Arguments" (pp. 329–33) and by doing several sample analyses in class. Once students are comfortable thinking critically about images in class, they will be more able to go off on their own to do critical analyses. You could also bring to class examples of good writing about images: short pieces of art criticism, incisive movie reviews, columns by popular cultural critics, and so forth. Use this analytical work to help them make better choices when they're producing their own visual arguments. If you have students work on the exercise from page 339, you might encourage them to bring in a presentation that they've done for your class or another setting. Our experience suggests that many students would do well to think more carefully about the visuals that they include in PowerPoint, Prezi, and other presentation media, and this chapter gives them the tools to think more carefully about their choices.

CHAPTER 15

Presenting Arguments

This chapter asks students to think about rhetoric as a set of tools that can help us shape our arguments in any number of different media; audience awareness, style, and appeals to ethos, pathos, and logos are important means of persuasion in any argument. If you have the time and flexibility, you might consider offering students the opportunity to present at least one argument for your class as something other than a traditional paper. When writing papers, students often cannot move beyond thinking of the instructor as the only audience for their writing. Using alternative means of presentation almost always forces student to think more fully about the audience to whom they might address their arguments, a step that usually results in higher-quality work.

Web sites present rich opportunities for rhetorical analysis: they usually contain textual and visual arguments; their organization can differ radically from print texts; and they face a potentially worldwide audience. Analyzing why some Web sites present more successfully than others will reward students when they make their own arguments in electronic environments: the tools of rhetoric will guide their decisions.

This chapter also offers a rhetorical approach to spoken arguments. Writing courses are increasingly being called on to address speaking abilities, and persuasive, skillful oral presentation needs to be learned and practiced as surely as written presentation does. Even when you're not working on oral presentations, you might ask students to read aloud some of their work or sample arguments from other sources. Ask students to read carefully, perhaps even somewhat dramatically. They'll learn a great deal about how style helps create an argument, and you'll benefit from learning more about how they hear language.

Respond

From pages 345, 359, and 364:

These exercises ask students to examine other arguments and figure out what makes them successful or unsuccessful. Have students bring their notes on these arguments to class and work in small groups to discover what similarities or differences in strategies they identified. Were the strategies and their successes determined by audience, personal preference, or something else? Can they derive general principles from their observations?

From page 352:

Make sure that students take no more than four paragraphs of a written essay to work with. You might suggest that they enlarge the type and increase the line spacing when they rewrite the text for oral argument. These changes will allow the student to highlight certain words and insert reminders to pause or slow down, ask for questions, or offer extratextual comments.

CHAPTER 16

Academic Arguments

All too often, instructors do not make their writing expectations as explicit as they should, and as a result students can adopt ponderous prose to "sound smart" or write like a professor. This chapter can give students the keys to the kingdom: once they recognize the features of academic writing, they're far more likely to be successful writing across the curriculum. They may not greet this chapter with great joy at first, so remind them that mastering the principles of this chapter will help them throughout their college career.

Even though the standards for academic argument are high, students shouldn't be intimidated by the prospect of writing for academic audiences. They do not have to become the world's expert on a particular topic to display an appropriate and impressive level of expertise: encourage them to use this chapter to familiarize themselves with the conventions of academic argument. Understanding the features of academic argument can prepare them for successful writing across the curriculum and help change their minds about some of the myths of academic writing.

Indeed, you might stress with students that academic argument is not merely a set of tricks and steps like avoiding contractions and split infinitives—two grammatical points that students have often learned as hallmarks of formal writing—but instead a way of thinking seriously and responsibly about almost any topic. You may not need to spend a great deal of time on this chapter, but students will surely return to it again and again; they will probably find the breakdown of academic arguments and the model arguments helpful in their own writing.

Respond

1. Look closely at the following five passages, each of which is from an opening of a published work, and decide which ones provide examples of academic argument. How would you

43

describe each one, and what are its key features? Which is the most formal and academic? Which is the least? How might you revise them to make them more—or less—academic?

Judith Thurman establishes her authority by reviewing what is known about the topic of cave paintings but does not seek to create new knowledge about the topic. Thurman uses a clear and formal style and makes mostly logical appeals. Including more formal citations would make this argument more academic.

Harry Crews is authoritative and uses a clear style, but he's writing about the topic of hitchhiking informally and not seeking to write about the topic in the way that, say, an academic sociologist might. To revise this into a more academic argument, a writer would more clearly identify what issues are at stake for a group of experts, seek out other sources besides personal experience, and opt for a more formal tone.

Elizabeth Derse's study of nitrogen sources is the most academic of the five passages. To revise the text into a less academic argument, a writer might offer a narrative that details personal experiences exploring and researching coral reefs, eliminate academic sources and citations, and perhaps use more emotional appeals about the importance of coral reefs and the dangers of degradation.

Jason Castro's argument popularizes academic argument for a serious, informed audience but not an audience of peer experts. To make this a more academic argument, a writer might cite sources and provide bibliographical information and seek to sound more authoritative (rather than questioning).

Dagoberto Gilb's argument is relatively informal, does not seek to deal evenhandedly with an opposing point of view, and relies heavily on emotional appeals. To revise this into a more academic argument, a writer might review what is known about the topic in a less partisan way, include more logical appeals based on research, establish a more objective ethos, and use a less conversational tone.

2. **Answers will vary. You may need to help students locate appropriate academic arguments. If possible, consider devoting some class time to showing students how to access scholarly databases on a library Web site, or consider**

scheduling a workshop with a reference librarian if that option is available.

3. Read the following three paragraphs, and then list changes that the writer might make to convert them into an academic argument.

The writer might approach this topic from a more academic point of view by reviewing academic opinions about the decline of reading rather than relying on the serious but not especially academic book by the critic David Ulin; by using a more formal style, especially in the first paragraph, which relies on several instances of informal figurative language ("chewed," "gored," "weapons of mass distraction"); by providing evidence of more rigorous research (and perhaps less reliance on appeals to personal experience in the last paragraph); and/or by including citations of sources used to build the argument.

4–5. **Answers will vary.**

CHAPTER 17

Finding Evidence

First-year writers can sometimes believe that "real" evidence is *always* statistical or quantitative. When you show your students that they have a wide range of sources and forms available to them, their arguments will probably improve. This chapter is probably best taught in conjunction with a larger unit: combine a discussion of evidence with an assignment to write an evaluative argument, for instance.

Once you explain to your class that evidence can take many forms (a good opportunity to review ethos, pathos, and logos), you can move on to a discussion of the inventional role evidence can take: finding one piece of evidence can lead students not just to other pieces of evidence but also to new ways of making their arguments. Searching for evidence in libraries, interviews, or observations is not simply a one-way activity that goes from one source to the next. Instead, it can help students understand what claims they want to make, how they can approach the argument, and how they should tailor their arguments to an audience.

First-year writers have often not yet chosen a major, but they might have some interest in a particular field or discipline. You could ask your students to interview faculty in their chosen field to find out what counts as evidence in that discipline. Students could then present their findings to the class. This is a two-part lesson: students have to *find* evidence *about* evidence.

Respond

1–4. These exercises focus on the inventional role of evidence gathering in addition to the technical questions of how to find evidence. If you'd like to teach your students research techniques, you might, if possible, display your library's online catalog page to show them how to get to research databases and how to use them. It's also probably a good idea to schedule a day in the library to walk around the reference areas and experiment with the catalog or, even better, to ask the librarians if they offer a guided tour or tutorial for students. Technical research skills are valuable, and first-year students rarely learn them except in their writing classes. And we've found that even some students who claim to know how to access databases benefit from seeing an instructor display how to work with them.

Exercises 3 and 4 focus on how to think about the evidence that students have found. Exercise 3 is especially useful for reinforcing the idea that evidence needs to be audience-appropriate. It's important for students to recognize that all types of evidence have contexts in which they won't work as well. Exercise 4 helps students understand how flexibility and the willingness to follow their research where it goes can significantly improve their arguments.

CHAPTER 18

Evaluating Sources

Many students have to struggle to write their own thoughts and arguments, so integrating others' ideas is a real challenge. Even just assessing sources can also be a challenge for students. Because the Internet makes finding material so easy, some students will be satisfied with the thousands of hits they get on any search. You will have to teach your students to be very critical of Internet sources: for example, a personal homepage on legalizing marijuana is significantly less credible than refereed research on hemp agriculture, but your students might not see the difference. The chapter includes a list of questions students can ask to determine the quality of any source, electronic or not.

Respond

1–3. The exercises focus largely on practicing how to assess authority and credibility in sources. The chapter describes the differences among quotations, paraphrases, and summaries. Students will probably benefit from practicing these techniques throughout the course, though the more context you can give them, the better. Rather than ask for summaries or paraphrases that are unrelated to students' long writing assignments, suggest that students write paraphrases or summaries in preparation for their other work—many of your students have probably written annotated bibliographies before, and these exercises are really versions of annotated bibliographies with more emphasis on assessment and less on summary. Alternatively, you could ask students to compile a "first-pass" bibliography on a given topic and then to make a second pass, evaluating the sources for inclusion in a shorter list. The more you integrate assessment of sources into the larger concerns of a course by tying the practice to projects that the students are working on, the more likely the exercise will pay off with improved use of source material for both you, the already overburdened reader of their texts, and the students.

Remind students to take special care when researching online, as it's easy to surf through multiple sources without taking thorough notes about where you've been and when you were there. We still come across many students every year who somehow believe that the Internet is actually only an extension of their own brain, a giant source that doesn't have to be cited. Some students will also need a reminder that they haven't exhausted all the possibilities for sources available to them if they stop with the first page of results from a Google search. Encourage them to use other databases and to look more deeply into the results to see what's available—even going to the second page of results on a Google search can open up new possibilities for some students.

CHAPTER 19

Using Sources

We have always found it disheartening when students bring us a draft of an argument and then say something like, "I still need to go back and find some quotations to put in there." This chapter can help them understand that sources and quotations need to be integral to the development of an argument, not just sprinkles dropped on top of an otherwise finished cake. Our experience is that students need this reminder more than once during a semester.

If your experience is anything like ours, your students might need special attention to the importance of framing quoted materials with signal words (pp. 426–27). We also think it's worthwhile to spend extra time discussing how many different ways writers can incorporate sources (pp. 428–31) since many student writers fall into the trap of believing that the only good sources are those that make precisely the same point or argument that the student wants to make. It's powerful and liberating for students to discover that they have the authority to disagree with or qualify the claims of others, rhetorical moves that are central to academic argument. We also think that teaching students to avoid "patchwriting" (pp. 432–33) is an especially important goal for a first-year writing class. Not only will this help students avoid plagiarism and academic dishonesty, but learning this concept and avoiding the practice will help students come to recognize themselves as authors and authorities, as writers who can earn the right to be trusted.

Respond

1–4. These exercises get students practicing the principles of using sources effectively. What we like best about using these exercises is that they give students concrete experiences in summarizing, paraphrasing, evaluating, and so on. It's hard to talk about using sources generally in a class discussion; our experience has been that students ask about theoretical situations that are hard to anticipate. These exercises will anchor your discussions about using sources in useful examples.

CHAPTER 20

Plagiarism and Academic Integrity

First-year writers have probably received some instruction in the concerns of intellectual property, and they're probably aware of the debates around movie and music piracy. They likely have heard of plagiarism in high school, have been taught not to copy others' work, and understand that plagiarizing is a form of cheating. But plagiarism is only a small part of the intellectual-property debate, and its parameters are far from well defined. You can help your students learn to use sources responsibly if you show them the range of activities that could reasonably constitute plagiarism, from simple copying of text without quotation or attribution to including images on a Web site that the student did not create. Students need to learn that intellectual property can be as jealously guarded as material property, if not more so: material goods can usually be replaced, but intellectual work is not easy to return.

The first-year writing class is usually the most important class for college students to learn to respect intellectual property rights and where they struggle with the boundaries of appropriate attribution. As the teacher, you can decide how strict to be with violations of intellectual property. Our experience has been that, for the most part, students do not intend to cheat or to copy without attribution.

In many cases, they have simply misunderstood the rules of attribution or have not thought carefully enough about their use of sources. If you use a process model in your course, you could encourage these students to write another draft, this time with appropriate use of sources. Another frequent cause of plagiarism is desperation. Students who wait until the night before an assignment is due are more tempted to cheat, which is another good argument for adopting a process model in your class; at the very least, require a short topic proposal and perhaps a partial draft. Of course, not all incidents of plagiarism are simply well-intentioned mistakes, but we argue for a generous conception of teaching in the first-year course. If students continue to violate the boundaries of intellectual property after you've been thorough in your instruction, you should take appropriate action.

Respond

1–4. The exercises for this chapter focus mainly on the differences among the various forms of intellectual-property protection. You could combine these exercises with a discussion of the protections available to people in different academic fields. For example, how do scientists in college biology departments protect their work? What about historians? How does each person build on previous work in the field without "copying"? Exercise 4 should be particularly useful for illustrating that intellectual property is as important an issue outside the classroom as it is inside it.

CHAPTER 21

Documenting Sources

Most of this chapter is concerned with the technical details of the MLA and APA citation systems, not with the way citation and documentation constitute a form of argument. The details are not hard to master, but they are complicated and require careful attention. Our experience has been that first-year students will make up their own citation systems—unfortunately, usually an inconsistent mix of dates, names, and titles—unless they are asked to follow MLA or APA guidelines carefully. Remind them that citation is largely a mechanical skill and that they need to use the models to learn how to format citations and bibliographies appropriately. Not many students need to memorize a citation system, and no one needs to memorize every possibility; they simply need to get comfortable with looking up the formatting and applying it correctly.

If you're teaching MLA format, you might talk about how MLA style attempts to minimize distractions to the reader by encouraging researchers to include authors' names in the text of the paper rather than just in the parenthetical citation and by placing most parenthetical citations at the ends of sentences. If you're teaching APA style, you might discuss how including the date of publication in a citation makes an argument about the importance of recent work. Part of the goal of teaching citation, after all, is teaching students that a documentation style is not just a random collection of rules but a system designed to make intellectual inquiry open and honest.

It's hard to design a class period that discusses citation in a way that's exciting for all students, but we strongly recommend that you review what you find most essential about citation format and perhaps demonstrate a few examples or have students practice a few examples in class. If students know that you're paying attention to the details, they're more likely to take the citation process seriously and not rely on vague memories of how they cited sources in high school. For example, every year we still have several first-year students who insist on inserting a comma between the author and the page number in in-text MLA citations even though MLA format does not call for it; for some students, the habits of high school are hard to break. Make your expectations clear and students will be more likely to respect the process.

Respond

1. This exercise asks students to identify the ways certain citation systems make arguments in themselves. Draw your students' attention to the relative placements of author, date of publication, and title in MLA and APA styles. You could ask your students to develop alternative citation styles that reflect some other values or priorities: How would they cite sources if they were concerned primarily with the author's credibility? Would book sales ever be an appropriate measure to cite in a bibliography?

2. This exercise allows students to practice citing works (e.g., songs) that they might be surprised to learn are covered by MLA and APA. This exercise should be fairly quick and simple for students, but make sure that they take the time to get their citations correct. No one has to enjoy the citation process, but they need to pay careful attention to be responsible and accurate.

CHAPTER 22

How Does Popular Culture Stereotype *You?*

Through the media—newspapers, magazines, radio, television, films, and the Internet—we regularly encounter stereotypes of various groups in our society. Whether based on some measure of reality or not, these stereotypes become part of our cultural folklore, and many people's perceptions of ethnic and social groups are based solely on representations they see in the media. How do we know when a representation will be accepted as tongue-in-cheek, ironic, or offensive, or even perceived as true?

- Do the media represent people as ideal types—that is, as we wish we were or as others (marketers? groups with various kinds of social power?) wish we were? If so, to what extent are these practices harmful? To whom? Why?
- Do the media represent some segments of the population in terms of ideal types and other segments in terms of stereotypes? If so, to what extent are these practices damaging? To whom? Why?
- When do the media influence us directly? When are they mediated in some way—that is, linked to complex changes that, in turn, influence attitudes or behaviors?

Stephanie Hanes *Little Girls or Little Women? The Disney Princess Effect* pp. 482–88

1. As Hanes represents the "Disney Princess Effect," what is it, and why does it matter?

The "Disney Princess Effect" is a shorthand description of the cultural and social forces that encourage girls to believe that their highest aspiration should be to resemble a Disney princess: attractive and ready to be taken care of by a man.

55

What other cultural trends is it related to?

Hanes argues that the Disney Princess Effect is related to a trend of sexualizing girls at young ages and of defining women entirely by their sexual attractiveness.

According to Hanes's characterization of the situation, who or what might be responsible for the increasing sexualization of little girls?

Hanes argues that the increasing sexualization of little girls mostly results from the proliferation of media images that emphasize sexual presentation and marketing pressures that encourage girls to consume formerly adult products such as makeup at earlier and earlier ages.

2. In its online form, the original article included a link to an online photo gallery: http://bit.ly/t8qkxP. Examine these photos and their captions. Do they merely illustrate the article, or are they providing particular kinds of support for the claims it makes? Which photo(s) and caption(s) do you find most effective?

   Answers will vary, but we would point to the photo reproduced on page 485 of the book as an example of a photo that provides support for the claims of the article. As the caption makes clear at the Web site, the girl in the photo is only ten years old, but the shoes seem like a much more adult option.

3. Hanes uses statistics along with other kinds of evidence in interesting ways to support her claims. (Often, arguments about this topic in the media rely primarily on personal experience or analyses of a few cases.) Find three or four statistics Hanes cites that gave you pause—that surprised you a bit—and be prepared to share these, to talk about your response, and to explain the value of using statistics effectively when discussing topics that are often discussed only in terms of personal experience.

   Answers will vary.

4. Visit Mary Finucane's blog, "Disney Princess Recovery: The Aging 8 Year Old": http://bit.ly/gIwa2H. Pay special attention to the "Welcome" information on the right-hand side of the page. How accurately has Hanes characterized and represented Finucane's

stance or position toward sexualization? What evidence can you provide for your evaluation?

Answers may vary. We would suggest that Hanes does not mischaracterize Finucane but that Hanes's article develops the idea of the sexualization of girls far more than Finucane does. For example, Finucane is certainly concerned about the sexualization of young girls; note that her subtitle is "Bringing Sexy Back for a Full Refund." However, Finucane focuses on how her daughter is less imaginative after exposure to the Disney princesses, not how she became more sexualized. For evidence that Finucane is not as concerned with sexualization as Hanes, we would cite the four scenarios she highlights that gave her concern ("Rigidity in Role," "Helpless Heroine," "Rapunzel Syndrome," and "Dress Drama").

5. Writing assignment

Classroom Exercise: focus on the world

Our experience is that many students can speak to the influence of Disney in their lives. Ask your students to study clips from Disney films or the lyrics from Disney songs to see how these pieces creature cultural expectations about gender. Does Disney seem dangerous to them? Do their favorite movies put forward arguments about gender identity that they find uncomfortable or, alternatively, inspiring? What do they see as the cultural work of Disney films?

Skip Hollandsworth *Toddlers in Tiaras* pp. 490–99

1. What argument(s) is Hollandsworth making in this article?

Hollandsworth argues that children's beauty pageants are wasteful, bizarre, and probably dangerous for young girls, particularly for their self-image.

How clear and explicit is his own stance or position toward the pageants he describes? What evidence can you give to support your responses?

We think his stance is fairly clear, and we would cite as evidence his repeated implication that the pageants do not lead to much promise of future success (see paragraphs 35–37, for example), his description of the expense of pageants

(see paragraphs 33–34, for example), his quotations from experts who disapprove of pageants and none who approve of them (see paragraphs 18 or 23, for example), and also the introduction of the idea that pageants would appeal to pedophiles (see paragraphs 12 and 13, for example). Answers, however, may vary.

2. Consider this article and the previous selection, Stephanie Hanes's "Little Girls or Little Women? The Disney Princess Effect." Both treat similar sets of issues and even use some of the same sources of evidence, for example, the work of journalist Peggy Orenstein. Are there other similarities?

We would suggest that both articles approach the subject with a seemingly neutral tone but manage to communicate strong disapproval of the culture of appearances and beauty that modern American girls are experiencing.

How do the two articles differ with respect to tone, kinds of evidence cited, and arguments made?

Hollandsworth's article is less objective and relies more on personal narratives of experiences with pageants. Hollandsworth's article is also about what he clearly perceives to be an odd subculture, whereas Hanes's article focuses on a particular issue that she believes has become part of mainstream culture.

To what degree might intended audience help account for these differences? As noted, *Good Housekeeping* is characterized as a women's magazine, and the path to the online version of this article is HOME > FAMILY & RELATIONSHIPS > PARENTING TIPS while the Christian Science Monitor is generally seen as an online newspaper that presents objective and, what one source terms, "nonhysterical" coverage of the topics it discusses.

Hollandsworth's article would probably appeal to an audience of parents who can feel good about themselves for not subjecting their own children to the bizarre (according to Hollandsworth) rituals of child beauty pageants. Hanes's article has a more sociological approach, as though she were diagnosing modern American culture.

3. How should we interpret this comment? Should we assume that DeMatteo recalls exactly what she said or the context in which she

said it? Should we assume that Hollandsworth misinterpreted or misrepresented DeMatteo's exact words or what they meant in context? If we take DeMatteo's comments at face value, assuming that her version of what she said represents what she said during the interview, how might that influence our evaluation of the article?

Answers will vary. DeMatteo probably remembers what she said, at least mostly, but she may, in retrospect, want to qualify, limit, or further explain her earlier words. Certainly Hollandsworth has to choose which quotations he will include, and he chooses lines that he thinks will help advance his thesis.

Of Hollandsworth's credibility?

This comment may make some readers distrust Hollandsworth as someone who twists the words of his subjects to suit his needs, but some readers will think that DeMatteo simply didn't want to sound so extreme in her comments about pageant life.

What might this example teach us about the challenges of working with sources generally, especially those from interviews we conduct?

Generally, this example should teach us that all communication comes with a context and changing that context can change the meanings of the words.

4–5. Writing assignments

Classroom Exercise: focus on rhetoric

Much of Hollandsworth's argument comes through narrative, a form of argument that can be more difficult for students to follow and even more difficult for them to produce. You might have them practice creating argument through narrative by having them tell the same story twice, each time with a different goal in mind. For example, ask a student to write the story of his or her life with himself or herself as the hero of the story. Then, using basically the same biographical details, have the student reframe the story with himself or herself as a victim. (You can also have students tell each other their life stories this way, an activity that takes only a few minutes.) This exercise exemplifies how choosing different interpretations of the same details turns narratives into arguments.

Ellen Goodman *The Culture of Thin Bites Fiji* pp. 502–3

1. What is Goodman's argument?

She argues that popular culture teaches girls and women to hate and harm themselves.

How does she build it around Becker's study while not limiting herself to that evidence alone? (Consider, especially, paragraphs 15–17.)

She does it by framing Becker's study within her own prose. She opens with an invitation to her readers to imagine a situation that sets up the background for describing Becker's research. She concludes by pulling back and adding her own commentary and recontextualizing the discussion in terms of the Columbine school killings.

2. What knowledge of popular American culture does Goodman assume that her *Boston Globe* audience has?

She expects them to have familiarity with popular TV shows, knowledge of the high incidence of eating disorders among young women, and awareness of incidents of killings in schools by young male students.

How does she use allusions to American TV programs to build her argument? Note, for example, that she sometimes uses such allusions as conversational asides— "All that and these islanders didn't even get *Ally McBeal*," and "At this rate, we owe the islanders at least one year of the ample lawyer Camryn Manheim in *The Practice* for free"—to establish her ethos. (For a discussion of ethos, see Chapter 3.)

Answers will vary. One strong possibility is that Goodman invokes shared knowledge to establish credibility with her audience and develop her ethos as someone in touch with popular culture.

In what other ways do allusions to TV programs contribute to Goodman's argument?

They provide specific evidence of the material viewed by Fijians.

Would you have understood this article without the glosses to *Ally McBeal* and *The Practice* that the editors have provided? What does this situation teach you about the need to consider your audience and their background knowledge as you write? (See Chapter 6 for a discussion of audience.)

Answers will vary, though if students do not understand the allusions then they would probably learn that they need to be aware of their audience's cultural knowledge and perhaps explain allusions or references that they make.

3. At least by implication, if not in fact, Goodman makes a causal argument about the entertainment industry, women's body image, and the consequences of such an image. What sort of causal argument does she set up? (For a discussion of causal arguments, see Chapter 11.)

She uses Anne Becker's research about teens in Fiji to argue about the effects of the entertainment industry on women's body image: teenage girls who watch popular American television shows develop a skewed image of the ideal female body size and shape.

How effective do you find it? Why?

Answers will vary.

4. Writing assignment

Classroom Exercise: focus on the world

Goodman's conclusion links eating disorders and recent school killings, stating that the media heavily influence adolescents to be destructive. How persuasive is this link? How similar are the two types of destructive behavior that Goodman cites—the destruction of others committed by certain boys and the self-destruction committed by certain girls? How is the role of the media similar in the two types of destruction? How is it different?

Anne E. Becker *Television, Disordered Eating, and Young Women in Fiji: Negotiating Body Image and Identity during Rapid Social Change* pp. 505–13

1. How does Becker link exposure to Western media to the changing notions young Fijian women have of their own bodies?

   The author interviewed young women in a rural town of Fiji three years after the introduction of television to the community. The social interviews focused on body image, and the researcher also analyzed the girls' references to media images.

   Why does Becker claim these women now want to be thin? How are these changes linked to other social changes occurring in Fiji, to adolescence, and to gender, especially in small-scale societies?

   Young women's focus has shifted from their communities' traditional values to the Western value of consumerism. They identify with television characters and celebrity lifestyles, and they equate too much weight with laziness and thinness with success. Fiji is also facing economic and social changes as it looks out onto a globalizing world. Young women are especially susceptible to these outside media forces in a climate of rapid social change when they are searching for role models. Women in general must consider self-presentation for social status in an environment where merit is ascribed, not achieved.

2. As Becker notes, she relies on qualitative data—specifically, interview data—to support her arguments. Why are such data especially appropriate, given her goals of understanding the changing social meanings of body image for young Fijian women as part of other rapid social changes taking place in Fiji? (For a discussion of firsthand evidence, see Chapter 16.)

   Interview data are firsthand evidence that may not be available through observations or even questionnaires. The perspective of a person involved in a specific situation is invaluable, especially in a changing social atmosphere where other types of evidence may be difficult to collect.

3. Throughout the Discussion and Conclusions sections, Becker repeatedly qualifies her arguments to discourage readers from extending them further than she believes her data warrant. Find two cases where she does so, and explain in the specific ways that she reminds readers of the limits of her claims. (For a discussion on qualifying claims and arguments, see Chapter 7.)

Answers will vary, but some examples include her use of "minimally" and "quite possibly." When Becker tells us that "Minimally . . . narrative data reflect a shift in fashion," she lets the reader know that her data report at least this fact and might have further implications. Her use of a qualifier in "Quite possibly . . . disordered eating may also be a symbolic embodiment of the anxiety and conflict the youth experience" suggests that the eating behavior of women is more complicated than a reaction to seeing beautiful people on television.

4. These excerpts from Becker's article represent research writing for an academic audience. What functions does each of the reprinted sections serve for the article's readers, and why is each located where it is? Why, for example, is an abstract placed at the beginning of an article? Why are keywords a valuable part of an abstract?

The delineated sections of the article give structure to the paper and create focal points for different information about the study. The abstract tells us what to expect from the paper as a whole, so it comes first. The discussion analyzes the data that have been presented. The conclusions draw the various points together with some implications for further research or action. The keywords present the main themes of the paper so that readers can judge the relevance of the article to the information that they seek.

5. Writing assignment

Classroom Exercise: focus on the argument

Becker reports that beauty standards are changing in Fiji due to the influx of Western ideals, specifically television images of slender women. Consider your response to this research. Would you have imagined that television could have such an effect in a culture with a long history of appreciating full-figured women? Is the problem that women want to be thin, or is their dangerous manner of losing weight the issue? Should one or both issues be addressed? Should young Fijian women be encouraged to return to their traditional beauty ideals? Using Becker's article as your source material, hold a debate or roundtable discussion in your class.

Sam Dillon *Evictions at Sorority Raise Issue*
of Bias pp. 515–18

1. What examples of stereotyping do you find in this article? Who is being stereotyped? What or who, do you believe, are the sources of the stereotypes?

   The women who were evicted from the house may have been stereotyped as uncool or "not sorority material." The description of the women from Indiana University as "plastic women" might serve as an example of a stereotype of those involved in Greek life.

   What evidence is there in the article of people who are criticizing or contesting stereotypes? Who are they, and how are they calling stereotypes into question?

   The women who are complaining about being moved to alumna status are criticizing and contesting stereotypes by suggesting that what matters in a good sorority is a diversity of women, not a certain look or social status.

2. Paragraphs 13–14 provide historical background about Delta Zeta sorority on the DePauw campus. Is this information necessary to the article? If so, how? If not, why not? What is the relationship between paragraphs 13–14 and paragraphs 15–16? What is the role of these two latter paragraphs in the article?

   Paragraphs 13 and 14 suggest a history of discrimination in this particular sorority, especially on the part of the national office. The information is not strictly necessary and may be read as either useful background or an unfair reminder of a distant past. Paragraphs 15 and 16 suggest some differences between the local chapter and the national office over the past few years, as these paragraphs suggest that the local chapter has a recent history of being inclusive.

3. In printed newspapers, corrections appear several days after the original article is printed, but someone doing research might well

not notice them. In contrast, a correction posted on an electronic source will always be available to future readers. In some cases, the correction is incorporated into the original article rather than being noted separately at the end of the article. The correction that appears at the end of this article reminds us that even award-winning journalists sometimes make errors. How serious, in your opinion, was the error in Dillon's original article? Does this correction influence how you read or evaluate the article? Does it influence how you evaluate the ethos of the writer? (For a discussion of ethos, see Chapter 3.)

Answers will vary.

4–5. Writing assignments

Classroom Exercise: focus on the world

If your school has Greek organizations, what stereotypes do you see for individual organizations or for Greek life as a whole? Think about other student organizations on your campus—sports teams, religious groups, minority organizations, or majors from a particular school or department. Do you think that your campus stereotypes individuals? Can you make an argument about how stereotypes might be useful or even helpful on a college campus? Can you offer evidence that stereotyping causes real harm to individuals?

Jack Shakley *Indian Mascots—You're Out!*   pp. 520–22

1. What argument is Shakley making about stereotypes in the media and popular culture?

   Shakley argues that stereotypes are demeaning and disrespectful and should be avoided.

   What sorts of claims does he make to support his position?

   He primarily makes emotional claims about the importance of treating everyone with dignity and respect, and he also asserts his own authority by making his Muscogee/Creek heritage part of the article.

   What concessions does he make to those who might disagree with him?

   In paragraph 4 he conceded that the issue of team names and mascots is a relatively small issue. In paragraph 5 he

concedes that some Native American mascots have been around so long that they have practically lost their meaning. In paragraph six he concedes that even a strong majority of Native Americans report having no objections to Native American mascots; in paragraph 10 he conceded that Native American team names and mascots do not represent any kind of pressing danger or threat.

How does he use these concessions to strengthen his own position?

Shakley's concessions make him seem reasonable; his audience is unlikely to accuse him of overreacting, and they are therefore more likely to trust him.

2. What kinds of evidence does Shakley use to support his argument?

Shakley begins with a personal narrative about how he offended his mother by wearing a hat with a negative stereotype of a Native American. He also uses examples of how mascots perpetuate negative stereotypes of Native American culture (see paragraphs 7 and 8 in particular).

How effective are his historical examples? In other words, what response did you have when you read about the Braves' mascots of the 1970s, for example, or the two examples cited in the final paragraph?

Answers will vary.

Why might Shakley have chosen these examples? How do they represent pathetic appeals?

These examples include potentially offensive language that we are not used to hearing in formal discourse, so most audience members are likely to be surprised by these team names in a way that "Seminoles" can no longer be surprising for those who are used to hearing the word. Because these words are likely to shock some readers who will be surprised that any team could have names like this, they invoke an emotional response.

3. The case of the Florida Seminoles is an interesting one because Florida State University (FSU) and the Seminole Tribe of Florida have reached an agreement, albeit a controversial one, that permits FSU to continue using their mascot, Chief Osceola, and the team

name, the Seminoles. They were prompted to do so following a 2005 ruling by the National Collegiate Athletic Association outlawing "mascots, nicknames, or images deemed hostile or abusive in terms of race, ethnicity, or national origin." Investigate this specific case to find out about the details of the agreement and debates surrounding it. (One resource is "Bonding over a Mascot," by Joe Lapointe, which appeared in the *New York Times* in December 2006; see http://nyti.ms/rU83kM. As you read that article, pay careful attention to the ways in which stereotypes are themselves part of the terms of agreement.) Based on what you learn, be prepared to discuss how Shakley would likely critique the Seminole Tribe's agreement with FSU beyond what he says in this essay.

Answers may vary, but you can point students to paragraphs 5 and 6 as good starting points for moving beyond this essay.

4. Shakley refers to the National Coalition on Racism in Sports and Media (NCRSM), an American Indian organization formed in 1991. Visit the organization's Web site, http://bit.ly/7wrjxg, to learn more about this organization and its efforts to fight what it sees as negative stereotyping. In what ways does the NCRSM seek to fight the common argument by supporters of the status quo, that is, those who support keeping Native American mascots, nicknames, and images, that these latter are used to honor American Indians and their culture and should be taken as compliments rather than as insults?

The NCRSM argues that Indian mascots work against "the principle of justice" by using stereotypes and racist images. One of their key values is "the right to self-identification and self-determination," a right undermined by the perpetuation of stereotypes. They further argue that reducing human beings, and especially those who are part of a race that endured genocide, to mascots is demoralizing and demeaning.

5. Writing assignment

Classroom Exercise: focus on the argument

Does your university or college use an Indian logo or another ethnic logo? How about students' favorite professional teams? How do students feel about changing these names and mascots? Do they have suggestions of other names and images that satisfactorily represent the spirit of the school? Does changing the mascot somehow break the chain of tradition? Does it change the ethos of the institution? Do people in the community in which the students are studying think that the change would be worth the effort?

Porochista Khakpour *Reality TV Goes Where Football Meets the Hijab* pp. 525–29

1. What arguments is Khakpour making about how stereotyping works in American society and especially in the media?

   Khakpour suggests that stereotyping in American media begins by emphasizing the most outlandish characteristics of a group but then eventually makes everyone seem fairly average and mainstream.

   In what ways is she arguing for the benefits of reality TV, an often-maligned genre of popular media?

   Khakpour argues that reality TV, which seems to focus on freaks, actually exposes how mundane-seeming outsiders are. That is, reality TV now shows us that people who look or seem very different are actually "just like you and me" (paragraph 14).

2. Khakpour's discussion of television and popular media reflects themes common in the writing of recent generations of the children of immigrants to the United States. As she notes in the selections opening line, "If anything made me an American, it was television." What, specifically, did television teach Khakpour about how Americans see the world?

   Television taught Khakpour that Americans might not make heroes of those who were different, but Americans tolerated difference, even freakishness. In her words, she learned, "Of all places, America was a pretty O.K. place for freakdom."

   At the same time, as Khakpour also notes, she never saw her own family—or families like hers—represented on television. What lessons did she learn from that fact?

   Khakpour writes that she learned to think of herself as an outsider, a freak, or a villain.

3. Humor is always a two-edged sword, and misused, it does far more damage than good. Yet Khakpour uses humor quite

effectively. How, specifically, does she use humor? Who or what are the targets of her humor?

Khakpour primarily targets reality television's creators and its consumers. She uses humor to mock how the creators come up with ideas for reality shows ("designers! cooks! the Amish! dwarf grooms!" in paragraph 4) as absurd. She also uses humor to point out how those who watch reality shows enjoy the outlandish nature of the shows ("I caught myself longing for a drunken brawl, someone in the bed of someone they shouldn't be with, some pretty girl's big stink on a spiral staircase" in paragraph 14). In this case, the targets of her humor are the audiences who want something embarrassing to happen.

How does her use of humor enable her to critique American society without putting readers who are different from her on the defensive?

Khakpour treats reality television humorously, but she includes herself as a target of the joke. Like her audience, she too is watching reality television and enjoying it, even growing involved enough in watching one show that she describes herself "scouring the women of the cast for my hot mess of choice" (paragraph 15). (Also see the quotation from paragraph 14 in the previous question.)

4. From a different perspective, we might claim that Khakpour uses aspects of Rogerian argumentation as discussed in Chapter 7, specifically the ways that she finds common ground with readers whose lives my be different from hers in many regards. In addition to humor (see question 3), what other techniques does Khakpour use in discussing Muslims in America at a time when suspicion of Muslims continues to run high?

Most of all, she emphasizes that Muslims are American, and that they are like average Americans in most ways. For example, she cites as one of the "most maxi-Muslim" moments in _All-American Muslim_ the coach's decision to have football practice at night, reminding readers that Muslims participate in a distinctively American sport, football.

5–6. Writing assignments

Khakpour ends up defending reality television as a genre that allows us to understand and appreciate differences as normal. Do students agree with her understanding of reality television shows that focus on "freaks"? Can they cite examples where reality TV does harm by reinforcing stereotypes or representing groups or individuals as dangerously outside the mainstream? What kind of influence does reality television have in shaping how we think about what it means to be an American?

Making a Visual Argument: Cartoons and Stereotypes   pp. 531–33

1. How would you state the argument each cartoon is making? In particular, what position or stance is the cartoonist taking with respect to the topic of the cartoon? What evidence can you cite for your claim?

   Answers may vary. Some possible answers appear below:

   Diffee: This cartoon argues that there is a divide between Southerners and Northerners, and that Southerners cannot quite get rid of the idea that Yankees are always popping up to create problems for Southerners.

   Allie: This cartoon suggests that the Left lacks traditional family values (and might even prefer birth control to raising children) and does not understand or appreciate the difficult work of raising children.

   Tornoe: This cartoon argues that Iowa is, in fact, a more progressive state than New Jersey because of the acceptance of gay marriage and that stereotypes of Iowans as rural, backwards thinkers and of New Jersey residents as urban progressives may need to be reconsidered.

   Sorensen: This cartoon argues that the claim that the hoodie is an article of clothing that marks someone as dangerous is ridiculous.

2. Cartoonists who create single-panel cartoons like these face great challenges: they have limited resources and space to make their argument clear, and they must do so in a humorous way.

A key way they succeed is by paying careful attention to visual and verbal detail. Choose two of these cartoons you think are especially effective in this regard, and be prepared to explain to your classmates how the cartoonists have used visual images and words effectively in ways that support each cartoon's argument.

Answers will vary.

3. A common source of humor is the juxtaposition of things that normally do not occur together. Where do we see evidence of this strategy in each of these cartoons?

Among the possible answers: having a formally dressed human being emerge from a carnival game might be an example of juxtaposition. Tornoe juxtaposes a stereotypical rural, agricultural scene with the word "progressive" and with the idea of a gay couple. Jen Sorensen juxtaposes an innocuous piece of clothing, the hoodie, with people (Vikings, terrorists) and an animal (a bear) that could potentially be truly frightening (the bear with a hoodie that reads "Bruins" nicely juxtaposes sports loyalty with a wild animal).

4. How does each cartoonist rely on stereotypes to make his or her point? In other words, which stereotypes common in American society do we see represented in these cartoons, and how does each cartoonist represent them so that they are immediately identifiable by readers?

Among the possible answers: Diffee represents the Southern man as especially masculine, and potentially also especially aggressive, with a cowboy hat, a Western-style shirt, and a hammer in his hand, while the Yankee looks like a weak, stereotypical nerd (bald, glasses, bow tie, and suit jacket). In Allie's cartoon, the liberal has a stereotypical beard, ponytail (though his hair is thinning), and sandals, while the mother looks harried and almost overwhelmed by her active, rambunctious children. Tornoe's cartoon relies on rural stereotypes; his image recalls Grant Wood's _American Gothic_ painting by including the pitchfork, but he opts to use overalls to signal the rural stereotype. Sorensen offers stereotypical Vikings and terrorists

recognizable through headgear (the horned helmet and the turban) and jokes about hipsters, hip-hop fans, and college students as stereotypical hoodie wearers.

5. Writing assignment

Classroom Exercise: focus on rhetoric

What kind of audiences do these political cartoons invoke? Do they set out to change the audience's mind, or are they being produced for an audience who already agrees with the ideas behind them? What evidence can you cite in these cartoons to support your position? Do cartoons have certain advantages or limitations that make them more or less likely to appeal to various audiences?

Charles A. Riley II *Disability and the Media: Prescriptions for Change* pp. 535–43

1. In what ways does Riley contend that the media and popular culture wrongly stereotype people with disabilities?

   Riley contends that the media patronize people with disabilities by treating their disability as the only significant aspect of their identity and by focusing on the process of overcoming the disability to fit into mainstream society as the most significant achievement in their lives.

   What negative consequences follow from this stereotyping for such people? For those who do not have disabilities? Why?

   These stereotypes treat the disabled as less than fully human and in some situations may make their suffering seem almost desirable. Audiences often have their sympathies manipulated and misunderstand the nature of the disability. Audiences also sometimes develop a sense of superiority since they are not disabled.

2. How convincingly has Riley defined a problem or need, which is the first step in a proposal argument? (For a discussion of proposal arguments, see Chapter 12.)

   Answers will vary.

3. What is your response to "Appendix A: Guidelines for Portraying People with Disabilities in the Media"? Are you familiar with the practices that these guidelines seek to prevent? Do you find the

guidelines useful or necessary? Why or why not? What justification might be offered for why specific guidelines are important?

Answers will vary; especially if students think that Riley is obviously right or obviously wrong, press them to use reasons and warrants to explain their thinking.

4–5. Writing assignments

Classroom Exercise: focus on the argument

Anyone who has watched sports on television, and especially the Olympics, has seen stories about how athletes have overcome personal tragedies or grave health concerns. Do stories of overcoming adversity consistently reduce the subjects of these stories to plot elements instead of real people? What are the dangers of reducing people to what Riley calls "allegorical flatness"? Can students offer an argument defending stories of adversity, even those that rely on traditional storylines?

Patricia J. Williams *Are We Worried about Storm's Identity—or Our Own?* pp. 545–48

1. Rather than passing judgment on the decision Storm's parents have made not to reveal their baby's biological sex, Williams uses the case of Storm to pose what she terms a "philosophical" question (paragraph 5) although the question is not posed until later in the article. What specific philosophical question is Williams posing?

"What would it mean if we were forced to hold in abeyance that foundering loss we feel when we encounter the limits of the known?"

Can you put the question in your own words?

Answers will vary. One possibility: What would it be like if we were really able to accept not knowing something that seems like basic knowledge?

In light of her comments, how is this question and the accompanying discussion an argument? What kind of argument is it—one of fact, of definition, of evaluation, of cause, or a proposal? Why?

The selection asks us to entertain a new way of thinking, one that doesn't always demand defined categories. Essentially,

then, this is a proposal argument that explores arguments of fact (is gender a real concept?), definition (how do we define maleness?) and cause (*why* do we insist on defining these things?).

2. In presenting her argument, Williams uses a very common strategy, especially among writers and speakers in the humanities. She opens with an anecdote, a short account of something that happened (paragraphs 1–2), and then returns briefly to the anecdote as she concludes her remarks (paragraph 10). Read these three paragraphs; then, reread the entire essay. In what ways does this anecdote contribute to the essay?

   Though answers will vary, we would suggest that the anecdote illustrates how unconsciously we focus on gender differences, thus potentially encouraging us to recognize how much a part of our lives these distinctions are.

3. What does Williams mean by the title, "Are We Worried about Storm's Identity—or Our Own?" Obviously, at this point in Storm's life, the baby cannot appreciate what it means to be female or male or to be so labeled repeatedly. In what sense, then, does a concern with Storm's identity provide evidence that we all have a great deal invested in "our boxes, our neat cabinets of thought" (paragraph 7) and that we are profoundly uncomfortable when we can't fit people into them?

   A concern with Storm's identity seems to have very little relation to concerns about Storm; after all, in paragraphs 4 and 5 we learn that Storm's sex is only a mystery to those outside the family, plus the parents say that they will not reveal the sex "for now," suggesting that it's possible that Storm will never feel the effects of not having gender revealed. Therefore, the concerns about Storm's gender mostly likely reflect our own concerns about categories, not concerns about how the situation will affect the child.

4. Particularly if you found question 3 difficult, you should Google "Storm Stocker" and read the comments posted on various media Web sites in response to Storm's parents' decision. As you'll see, commenters generally responded very negatively to the story and gave strong evidence that they had much invested in a world

where everyone is either male or female and unambiguously so. Choose three or four of these comments you find especially interesting in terms of the argument(s) they are making, and be prepared to share them with your classmates and to explain the assumptions the arguments make as well as the reasons you find them interesting.

Answers will vary.

5. Writing assignment

Classroom Exercise: focus on the world

What responsibility do parents have to their children to make sure that the children's identity makes sense to those outside the family? Storm's parents obviously created quite a stir. If you found yourself objecting to their decision, what do you think about parents who raise their children inside a strict religious tradition or in any other tradition or subculture that might pull children out of the mainstream? To what degree does a child's identity belong to the parents' choices? (If you answer that anything is acceptable as long as parents don't harm the child, be sure that you explain what "harm" means in relation to building a child's identity.)

Jennifer Conlin *The Freedom to Choose Your Pronoun*   pp. 550–51

1. What argument(s) might supporters of preferred gender pronouns (P.G.P.'s) claim to be making and why?

   Supporters might claim to be arguing that gender is not a fixed category but a choice; that gender identity and sexuality are separate issues; and that gendered pronouns can be a way of limiting identities.

   What is your response to such arguments? Why, in your opinion, do you respond as you do?

   Answers will vary.

2. Supporters of PGP's are making complex assumptions about language—specifically, pronouns—on the one hand and identity categories, whether those related to biological sex, gender identity, or sexual orientation or identity, on the other. Using the discussion of Toulmin argumentation presented in Chapter 7, seek

to make as explicit as possible the argument(s) P.G.P. supporters are making about language and identity categories.

Answers will vary. We offer two suggestions:

Claim: Gender-specific pronouns are untrustworthy and potentially coercive.

Reason: Gender-specific pronouns restrict identity to one of two fixed options.

Warrant: Identity is a fluid, not a fixed, concept.

Backing: Identity should be determined by individuals, not by society.

Warrant: Human identity has more than two options.

Claim: Sexual identity is not personal identity.

Reason: Identity is complicated and varied.

Warrant: Identity should not be determined by forces outside the individual.

Warrant: Identity is a fluid, not a fixed, concept.

3. Comments posted in response to articles are often interesting places to see examples of critical reading and evaluation, especially in certain publications like the *New York Times*. If you can, you may wish to read the comments posted in the response to this article on the *New York Times* site, especially those labeled as "Highlights," a label indicating that the editors see these remarks as among the most thought provoking of those posted. Some commenters were critical of Dr. Savin-Williams because of the way in which, at least as represented here, he seemed to confuse issues of gender identity and sexual orientation or identity. Why might they make such a claim?

The article quotes Dr. Savin-Williams listing terms specifically about sexual orientation (see paragraph 6) as part of the evidence about their gender identity, even though earlier in the article Katy makes the distinction between these kinds of identity explicit (paragraph 3).

Why is keeping complex categories like these distinct especially important when constructing arguments?

This question might provide an opportunity for talking to students about quoting sources and using evidence. Is Dr. Savin-Williams confusing the terminology or is the author quoting in a way that confuses the terminology?

4. Another critique of the article was that some of the students quoted seemed to be prisoners of language and stereotypes themselves. As one commenter, cyncytee, who claimed to be posting in Cincinnati, wrote on October 1:

> Put me in the relatively intolerant column on this one. English pronouns distinguish male from female by "equipment," as the story puts it. That is not repressive. Over several generations, society has come to accept that physical gender does not—or should not, at least—determine one's life roles. That's for the better. Denying physical realities because of how one feels in the morning is ridiculous. How 'bout we just learn that hims and hers come with all sorts of vocal pitches and outward accouterments and that invoking old, gender-specific traditions doesn't make one that gender.

What responses might the supporters of P.G.P. offer to this critique of their assumptions and actions?

They might object that the commenter misses the point and that the pronouns that others use to describe us actually help determine our identities because they shape how others think of us and expect us to act. Further, the commenter assumes that the idea of two genders (as opposed to two sexes) is natural and fixed whereas their arguments suggest that recognizing only two gender identities may be limiting in itself.

5. Writing assignment

Classroom Exercise: focus on the argument

How flexible do you think gender or sexual identity is? Is it reasonable or silly or somewhere in between for someone to claim that sometimes he or she wakes up to feel like a different gender? Is gender identity really malleable enough to change frequently—how do you know that it is or isn't? What evidence can we cite to understand gender identity aside from our own experience? Do we need any evidence outside of our own experience?

Claude M. Steele *An Introduction: At the Root of Identity,*
from *Whistling Vivaldi and Other Clues to
How Stereotypes Affect Us*   pp. 554–65

1. How does Steele define the stereotype threat and its importance
   for all of us?

   **The stereotype threat is a kind of pressure on us to repre-
   sent a larger group of which we are a part in a particular
   way. It is important for all of us because it can affect anyone's performance on particular tasks and, therefore, our
   sense of identity, the choices we make in life such as what
   kind of work to pursue or who are friends will be.**

   What specific conclusions does he draw from his research and that
   of others on the stereotype threat and stereotypes more broadly?

   All from pages 564–65:

   **1. Despite our sense of ourselves as entirely autonomous,
   stereotypes shape our identities.**

   **2. Stereotypes and other identity threats contribute to
   larger social problems.**

   **3. Stereotypes and other identity threats can harm our
   brain activity and mental functions.**

   **4. Solutions and strategies exist for reducing the impact of
   threats from stereotypes.**

2. What specific functions does the lengthy quotation from an essay
   by Brent Staples (paragraphs 13–15) play in Steele's argument?

   **The quotation (1) describes a stereotype threat that affects
   his relationships with other people, (2) demonstrates how
   an identity contingency shapes who he is, and (3) also demonstrates a strategy that can reduce the stereotype threat.**

   Why could Steele simply not paraphrase or summarize Staples'
   discussion?

   **Paraphrasing the story would have negated the sense of
   narrative and drama; in particular, we would lose the sense
   of discovering a strategy for reducing the stereotype threat.**

What value is there for Steele in using a first-person example here? In using an example from someone else, rather than using another example of his own?

The first-person example makes the experience more immediate, and quoting someone else reminds us that Steele is not the only person to experience life this way; that is, quoting someone else helps establish the experience as typical rather than exceptional.

If Steele had been writing an essay of 500 words, how might he have used this quotation or information from it? Why?

In an essay of 500 words, Steele would have had to cut the quotation dramatically to keep it from overwhelming his own argument.

3. As noted in the headnote, if Steele were writing only for social psychologists, his primary support would come from quantitative evidence based on experiments. Here, however, Steele uses many sorts of evidence. What kinds of evidence does he use to support his claims?

Personal narratives, testimony, and anecdotes are all important forms of evidence for Steele.

How effective are they and why? (For example, is any of his evidence particularly memorable? What makes it so?)

Answers will vary.

4. Steele also uses definitions in very interesting and effective ways. How does Steele go about defining the following abstract nouns: *encounter, condition of life, contingency, intersubjectivity,* and *threats in the air.*

"Encounter"—in paragraph 1, context defines "encounter" as a moment of understanding how the world outside the self works to define one.

"Condition of life"—in paragraph 2, context defines a "condition of life" as a way of living one's life according to certain rules set by culture and circumstances and not subject to change simply by asserting one's individuality.

"Contingency"—in paragraph 6, defined as "circumstances you have to deal with in order to get what you want or need in a situation."

"Intersubjectivity"—in paragraph 10, defined as "the fact that as members of society we have a pretty good idea of what other members of our society think about lots of things, including the major groups and identities in society." In other words, "intersubjectivity" says that our identity is composed of ways that others think about us as well as how we experience our own identities.

"Threats in the air"—in paragraph 28, defined by the context as a kind of contingency that can "confirm a bad group stereotype as a characterization of their group and of themselves" for a minority.

How does each of these definitions contribute to the effectiveness of Steele's selection?

Answers will vary, but we would suggest that these definitions give his argument more academic credibility because he has identified a number of abstract concepts and explained them. On other hand, because his definitions are relatively informal, they also make his writing more effective because they are personal and easily understood.

5–6. Writing assignments

Classroom Exercise: focus on the argument

To what degree do you understand your identity in relation to a larger group? To what degree do others understand your identity in relation to a larger group? Have you ever felt pressured to act in a particular way or subscribe to a particular set of beliefs because of your ethnic, gender, religious, racial, national, or cultural identity? Is it possible to be entirely free of group identities, to be an entirely autonomous person independent of other identifying forces?

Wrap-up Exercises for "How Does Popular Culture Stereotype *You?*"

The following questions invite students to consider themes from the readings in this cluster. They can be used for extended projects as well as in-class essay questions.

1. Write a personal response to the issue of representations of groups. In your response, detail your understanding of the impact of images in the media on your own life. Do you see yourself and people like you (in any sort of way) represented in the media? If you do, where? How often? In what sorts of roles or situations? What are the consequences of these facts for you? For those like you? For those who are not like you? If you do not see yourself or others like you (in any sort of way) represented in the media, what are the consequences of that fact for you? For others like you? For those who are not like you?

2. This chapter explores how the media stereotype certain categories of Americans, especially minorities, and in most cases the readings suggest that stereotypes present a danger to individuals, to a group, or to the culture. Write an essay in which you examine the potential consequences of media stereotypes for society as a whole or for a particular group or person. Note that you might wish to argue that there are no negative consequences of media stereotypes or that, if there are, we should not be concerned with them. Your essay will likely be most successful if you are careful to qualify your claims and to cite specific evidence, rather than dealing in vague generalities.

CHAPTER 23

What's It Like to Be Bilingual in the United States?

The readings in this chapter focus on issues relating to language and its varieties, and how we decide when, where, and with whom to speak different languages. The readings remind us that issues of language and identity are all around us, in every conversation and every text. In all of these cases, language functions as a tool for communicating information about the world and as a symbol of who we—as speakers, signers, or writers—are or wish to be. Part of the meaning of any variety of language is its value in various linguistic "markets"—on the street, in communities where it is spoken, in communities where it isn't, in the classroom, on the basketball court, during prayers. The decision to use English or another language must take into account much more than simply which language one prefers.

If we take language as a prism through which to view identity (and hence society), we appreciate how challenging it is to negotiate common ground on which to construct our arguments about language. As these texts remind us, however, if thoughtful arguments about language are to take place, we have no choice but to struggle with these challenges. These texts also remind us of the need to engage in such arguments. In this regard, they show us that language is not different from many other sources of social difference in our society.

Hyon B. Shin and Robert A. Kominski
Language Use in the United States: 2007   pp. 571–93

1. How would you characterize the argument made by this selection overall? Is it an argument of fact, an argument of definition, an argument of evaluation, a causal argument, or a proposal? What evidence would you give for your claim?

**A factual argument. Students might cite the early descrip-
tion of the report as one "that presents population and
housing data" and one "that describes population distribu-
tions and characteristics." They might also cite the lack of
policy proposals or discussions of how to interpret or
think about the data.**

At the same time, can you find short passages that represent other
kinds of arguments in this selection? Give several examples.

Answers will vary. Among the possibilities:

**Definition argument: "People speaking at a level below the
'very well' category are thought to need English assistance
in some situations." (paragraph 6; while the assessments of
language ability are evaluative arguments, in this case the
argument establishes the definitional criteria for speaking
"very well": one does not need English assistance)**

**Causal arguments: "In the short term, the factors creating
these concentrations include points of entry into the United
States and family connections facilitating chain migration
(Palloni et al. 2003). In the longer term, internal migration
streams, employment opportunities, and other family situations help to facilitate the diffusion of language groups
within the country." (paragraph 25)**

**Evaluation argument: "Data on speakers of languages other
than English and on their English-speaking ability provide
more than just an interesting portrait of a changing nation.
Routinely, these data are used in a wide variety of legislative, policy, and research applications. Legal, financial, and
marketing decisions regarding language-based issues all
rely on information that begins with data on non-English
language use and English-speaking ability." (paragraph 3;
argues for the usefulness of the report)**

2. How does this report give us insight into the changing nature of
   bilingualism in the United States—not only the languages and
   groups involved, but also the places where languages other than
   English are likely found and reasons why?

   **The report offers information about how language patterns
   have changed over time, especially the decline of several**

European languages (Polish, Italian, and German, for example) and Yiddish and the explosive growth of Asian languages and Spanish. The report also reveals that the greatest growth in bilingualism has taken place in the Southwest and "immigrant gateway states" (paragraph 23).

Why, according to the report, are data such as those presented here useful and even necessary?

Paragraph 3: "Data on speakers of languages other than English and on their English-speaking ability provide more than just an interesting portrait of a changing nation. Routinely, these data are used in a wide variety of legislative, policy, and research applications. Legal, financial, and marketing decisions regarding language-based issues all rely on information that begins with data on non-English language use and English-speaking ability."

3. This report was produced by the U.S. Census Bureau. How does that fact itself represent an ethical appeal? For example, how might it influence your evaluation of the credibility of this report as a source you might use for constructing an academic argument? How does the section titled "Source of the Data and Accuracy of the Estimates" (p. 589) represent an ethical appeal? (For a discussion of ethical appeals, see Chapter 3. For a discussion of evaluating sources, see Chapter 18.)

The U.S. Census Bureau, having had its purpose outlined in the Constitution, has long had a reputation as a responsible, nonpartisan organization, though political groups have certainly challenged that nonpartisan stance. The U.S. Census Bureau is likely to seem very credible for an academic argument because of its long history and its nonpartisan reputation.

4. Compare the information given in Table 4 and Figure 3. Both present information about the population aged five or older who were reported to speak a language other than English at home by state in 2007. What information do both present?

Both present statistics on the percentage of the population who spoke a language other than English at home broken down by state.

What additional information is presented in Table 4?

Table 4 also reveals the English-speaking ability of the respondents.

What does the presentation in Figure 3 make evident that the presentation in Table 4 cannot show us?

Figure 3 makes it evident that the highest percentages of those who speak a language other than English at home are concentrated in the Southwest, from California to Texas, and that states with large urban populations also have higher percentages of residents speaking a language other than English at home.

What do these two presentations of the data—and in some cases, the same data—remind us about the nature of visual arguments? (For a discussion of visual arguments, see Chapter 14.)

Visual arguments, like all argument, represent a series of choices of what to emphasize and what to leave out, so how a visual argument is designed will determine, at least in part, what argument it makes.

5. Study Appendix A carefully. As noted, it provides the questions that have been used about language in the U.S. census as far back as 1890, when the first questions were asked. As should be clear, the questions have not been consistent, and many decades, no questions were asked about language at all. What problems does this situation create for researchers who wish to understand changing patterns of language use in this country?

The questions asked determine to a significant degree the answers that will be given, so if the questions change over the years, so will the way that people respond. As a result, researchers cannot rely on the evidence to be consistent, making it harder to track changes in language use over time.

What consequences does it have for the country as a whole?

The change in question leads to a change in answers: as a result, our understanding of the history of what languages were spoken in the United States can become distorted,

which may affect our decision making about political and economic policy.

Classroom Exercise: focus on rhetoric

The U.S. Census Bureau "collapses languages into smaller sets of 'language groups,'" and one of these groups, oddly, is "Spanish" (paragraph 4). How do you respond to this category? Can you come up with other ways that the Census could divide languages into categories? In what other places in this report does the Census Bureau have to make choices, perhaps unexpected, in order to organize large amounts of data? How does the need to shape the data create a kind of argument?

Sandra Cisneros From *"Bien Pretty"*   pp. 596–97

1. For Cisneros—and one can likely claim it for all bilinguals—in some sense the languages she knows aren't equal. Rather, each language is associated with different worlds of experience. What does Spanish connote for the narrator in Cisneros's text? What does English connote? Where would such connotations come from?

   Spanish connotes memories from home and family life because it is the language she grew up with, the language spoken inside her home. English has harsh, stiff connotations, "starched *r*'s and *g*'s" (paragraph 5), likely because she grew up with it being used for official business with those outside of her family and community.

2. One resource bilingual writers have is code switching—switching between the languages they know. In this excerpt, we see the simple noun phrase "la Alhambra" (paragraph 4) from Spanish, which we can correctly understand even if we know no Spanish. We also see the phrase "*Ya, ya, ya*" (paragraph 9), which is followed immediately by the English equivalent, "There, there, there." Yet we also find the phrases "*mi vida, mi preciosa, mi chiquitita*" (paragraph 4), which we may not be able to figure out the meanings of. (In fact, the phrases translate literally as "my life, my precious [one], my dearest little [one]"—things native speakers of English wouldn't normally say to one another, even when being intimate. Such phrases are perfectly normal among

speakers of Spanish.) Why might writers purposely create texts that include parts readers may not be able to understand? Why would such a strategy be especially effective when talking about intimacies like making love?

Writers might use code switching to mirror their normal speech patterns among bilingual friends and family. In addition, they might want to leave some elements of their story out of their reader's comprehension. For Cisneros, lovemaking remains a private act because her English-speaking readers cannot understand Flavio's sweet nothings.

3. Writing assignment

Classroom Exercise: focus on style

Using Chapter 13 (Style in Arguments) as a guide, analyze Cisneros's use of figurative language. How does she use literary tropes such as metaphors, similes, and analogies to make her writing more compelling? How does she use syntactic schemes for the same purpose? What sentences, phrases, paragraphs, or ideas do you find most striking? Why? How does her writing style affect your reading, understanding, analysis, and evaluation of her argument?

Marjorie Agosín *Always Living in Spanish*   pp. 599–601

Marjorie Agosín *English*   pp. 602–4

1. Why does Agosín write only in Spanish? How do her reasons for using Spanish compare with those of Cisneros? How does she regard using Spanish as relating to her ancestry as a Jew?

   She writes only in Spanish to keep the memories of her childhood alive. She and Cisneros both see Spanish as connected with their families, with their community, and with their homes. Growing up in a Jewish family that was forced to flee, Agosín sees language as a key to memory, often the only way to remember what you were forced to leave behind.

2. What sort of experiences did Agosín have while trying to learn English? How typical do you think her experiences were? In other words, how do Americans who are native speakers of English

treat non-native speakers of English? How did Spanish represent a source of strength and consolation to Agosín during the period when she was learning English?

She was ridiculed and insulted, and she constantly felt the need to explain to English speakers why her English was so poor. She was treated as an outsider and given less respect than a native speaker of English was given. Spanish was a strength and consolation because it connected her with her identity, the world she left behind, the security of her family, and the space in which she belonged.

3. What does Spanish represent for Agosín? Why would it represent these things for her?

Answers will vary but might include the notion that Spanish represents many of her memories from Chile—plants and flowers, family, friendship, warmth. It represents these things because it's connected to her memories of childhood and to her nostalgia for the country and family she left behind.

4. Writing assignment

Classroom Exercise: focus on the argument

How is Agosín's poem similar to and different from her essay? How does one text help you understand the other? What argument does each make? Do you think one is more effective than the other? Why? Why would the editors of this textbook choose to include both the essay and the poem?

Firoozeh Dumas *The "F Word"* pp. 605–8

1. How might you summarize Firoozeh Dumas's argument? What is its subject—the importance of names, the ways in which Americans have traditionally responded to unfamiliar names, the immigrant experience, all of these?

Dumas's argument is that a name is an integral part of human identity. The subject of the article is how Americans respond to names and what they assume from names. This look at names is interesting because it's from an immigrant's point of view.

2. Carefully reread paragraph 12, in which Dumas explains how having an "American" name and speaking English without a foreign accent was like having "X-ray glasses." Is Dumas's portrayal of Americans in this passage and elsewhere in the essay flattering? Humorous? Honest? Dumas notes that "people assumed I was American." What definition of "American" must she (and those she writes about) be assuming?

Dumas talks about certain people's responses to her when assuming she was American. These people and those who avoid pronouncing foreign names (Americans) are not portrayed in a positive light. "American" is conversely broadened to apparently mean someone born in the United States who speaks English without an accent.

Is such a definition valid, given evidence she presents elsewhere in the essay and the fact that the United States is often called a nation of immigrants? At what point does an immigrant become an American?

Answers will vary.

3. How would you describe Dumas's use of humor? Find three examples that you especially like, and explain how the humor helps the author achieve her goals. In what ways does Dumas's argument represent satire, with the simultaneous goals of ridiculing and remedying a problematic situation? (For a discussion of the uses of humor in argumentation, see Chapter 2.)

Answers will vary.

4. How does Dumas use the repeated metaphor of the spice cabinet to help structure her argument? Why is this metaphor an appropriate one, given her topic? How does the metaphor permit her to critique the mother who called her "F Word" (paragraph 17)?

The metaphor of spice can be used to talk about the sounds of language, cultural experiences, comforts, and the willingness to try new things. This usage is particularly appropriate for her topic and allows her to accuse the mother from her children's school of refusing to add to her spice cabinet.

5. Writing assignment

Have students ever chosen a new name in a language class? How did they feel about that? Have they ever traveled to a foreign country and changed the pronunciation of their name or chosen a whole new name to make other people feel more comfortable? To fit in better? Have they chosen to keep their own name even when the pronunciation is very different from the host language? Was it frustrating to hear their name presented so differently? What is it about our names—which are just words, after all—that hold so much personal identity and meaning?

Making a Visual Argument: Public Service Announcements in Spanish

National Institute of Mental Health
En la comunidad latina tenemos una
cultura de silencio   p. 611

Ad Council *Hija, debes ir a la universidad*   p. 612

1. These ads appear in English and Spanish versions. (In fact, the ad about depression includes the tag line "Real Men. Real Depression" in English, an example of code switching of a sort one wouldn't likely see if these ads were in a country where Spanish is the major or official language.) How do language choice and intended or invoked audience interact in these advertisements?

   This advertisement invokes a Latino or Hispanic male audience in America, and the language choices reflect an assumption of at least some bilingualism in the audience. That is, as the question suggests, even the small amount of English included reflects that the audience is not in a country where only Spanish is spoken.

   Many U.S. Latinos are highly bilingual, although some of them prefer English, some prefer Spanish, and others have no preference. On the other hand, some Hispanic Americans speak little or no English, and still others speak little or no Spanish. How does this situation complicate efforts to create advertisements that target this community?

   The multitude of language preferences makes it hard to figure out how to appeal to the largest number of potential

audience members; every choice that one group will embrace might be rejected by another group.

2. Evaluate "En la comunidad latina tenemos una cultura de silencio" as an argument. What role does the personal testimony of Rodolfo Palma-Lulión play in the PSA? Does it matter that he is a university student? Why or why not?

   The testimony of Palma-Lulión allows the male audience to relate to him as another man. As a university student he represents someone who is educated and successful and yet struggles with depression.

   Why might the phrase "Real Men. Real Depression" appear in English?

   "Real Men. Real Depression" may be the official motto of the campaign to reach men in all languages. The subtle code switching invokes an audience of bilingual men.

3. Evaluate one or more of the ads created for the "Hispanic College Preparation" campaign as arguments. How do the images, sounds, and/or words work together to make an argument? How well is the argument motivated, given the justification that is cited for creating the campaign?

   Answers will vary, but be sure to require students to state their evaluative criteria explicitly: have them practice what they've learned in the class.

4. Some might criticize these U.S. government agencies or the Ad Council for producing advertisements in any language other than English. What arguments might they use for such criticisms? What costs, direct or indirect, might there be if U.S. government agencies do not produce PSAs in languages other than English?

   The agencies behind these ads use different languages to reach different audiences that need their help. Not addressing audiences who do not speak English would leave a large section of the population without services and could mean that more emergency services would be required in the future.

5. Writing assignment

Some argue that American advertisements and public-service announcements should be presented in English and that presenting them in other languages enables people to avoid learning English. Why would public-service agencies create a Spanish-language campaign? Why might a business make advertisements in other languages? Does this sound like a good business practice? How would you react to people from Miami or Los Angeles who felt that Spanish advertising was invading their cityscape?

Lan Cao *The Gift of Language*   pp. 615–20

1. What's your initial response to this excerpt from Cao's novel? Given the mother's cultural expectations, which she has brought from Vietnam, is it logical for her to respond as she does?

   Answers will vary.

   In what senses is Cao forced to parent her mother?

   She must teach her mother how to behave appropriately in the United States.

2. How does Cao construct the argument she makes here? What sorts of evidence does she rely on? How does she use language effectively to convey her ideas? (Chapters 7, 17, and 13, respectively, will help you answer these questions.)

   Cao uses specific incidents, such as their experience buying pork at the supermarket, to describe the process of immigrating and the effect it had on her relationship with her mother. She uses vivid descriptions of the American and Vietnamese markets to note their extreme differences.

3. The tale that Cao tells has been told many times in the writings of immigrants, especially those who arrive in the United States as children with parents who speak little or no English. What are the consequences for family life? How does language become a source of power for the child? How does this power disrupt traditional patterns of family life?

   Family dynamics shift. Children must grow up fast and be able to explain the ways of this new country to their

parents, and parents must accept the authority of their children.

4. Writing assignment

Classroom Exercise: focus on rhetoric

Although this is an excerpt from a novel, Cao makes a clear argument here. Conduct a Toulmin analysis of Cao's argument. What is her claim? What are her reasons? What are her grounds to support her claim? What are her underlying warrants, and what backing does she provide for them? Does she provide any qualifiers and rebuttals? Do you think her argument is effective or ineffective? Why? How does the fact that this is an excerpt from a novel affect your analysis of the argument?

Amy Tan *Mother Tongue*   pp. 622–27

1. How have Tan's attitudes toward her mother's English changed over the years? Why?

   She has learned that her mother's English is not "broken," and she is no longer ashamed. She understands that having language-learner's grammar or accent does not diminish the quality of her mother's thoughts.

   In what ways does Tan describe a situation that probably is faced by most children of immigrants?

   Many children of immigrants probably feel caught between two cultures, and their parents' difficulty with English may force them into situations and roles that they don't feel prepared for.

   In what ways is this situation like or unlike the embarrassment that children generally feel about their parents at some point in their growing up?

   Answers will vary.

2. Why is Tan suspicious of language ability tests? What are her complaints?

   She is suspicious of these tests because they can't measure richness of language use or of language perception. She is

uncomfortable because the test questions have only one correct answer, as though they are math questions.

What sort of evidence does she offer?

She uses an extended example of the limitations of analogy questions. These questions aim at only one specific relationship between two words even though there may be others. The person who perceives that richness is penalized.

Do you agree or disagree with her argument? Why?

Answers will vary.

3. Tan's text was written to be read aloud by the author herself. In what ways might this fact be important? (For a discussion of the features of arguments to be heard, see Chapter 15.)

Spoken texts require more and different signposts to help listeners keep track of the structure. They usually use simple sentences. Informal language is usually more acceptable in spoken texts.

What would it be like, for example, to have heard Tan deliver this text? How would such an experience have been different from reading it on the page? Had Tan written the piece to be read silently by strangers—as her novels are, for example—how might she have altered it? Why?

Answers will vary.

4. Writing assignment

Classroom Exercise: focus on rhetoric

Amy Tan and Lan Cao both write about their mothers and their mothers' language. Compare and contrast the ways in which these writers use their mothers' language and experiences with languages as part of their argument.

Twin Cities Public Television *First Speakers:*
Restoring the Ojibwe
Language   pp. 628–37

1. What argument(s) is each section of this program making?

Part 1, Introduction: This section presents an argument of fact that language extinction is taking place. It also

introduces arguments of definition (a language is a treasure or artifact) and arguments of evaluation (this and other languages with small numbers of speakers are worth saving).

Part 3, Immersion: This section contains a causal argument explaining why the Ojibwe language declined so much as well as evaluation arguments that argue for the value of immersion programs.

Part 5, Ponemah: This section contains arguments of fact establishing Ponemah's centrality to the Ojibwe language. We would argue that this section also contains an implied evaluation argument suggesting that a community that preserves the language will be a stronger community overall.

What function does each serve independently?

Answers will vary, but we suggest the following:

Part 1: Establishes a problem.

Part 3: Illustrates how the community is addressing the problem through education.

Part 5: Presents daily life in an Ojibwe-speaking community.

As part of the program as a whole?

Answers will vary, but we suggest the following:

Part 1: By setting up the problem, this section sets the stage for the rest of the program.

Part 3: Suggests a future for the Ojibwe language by focusing on the language's part in education.

Part 5: Suggests the value to a community of preserving the language.

2. Based on the information from readings in this chapter, how does the bilingualism in Native American communities differ from that found in communities of recent immigrants?

One difference is that Native American communities are often reclaiming a threatened language; they are not moving from one language community to another but rather re-creating a language community that had almost become extinct.

In what ways is it similar?

As with the immigrant groups, language provides an important marker of cultural heritage and identity for the speakers and the members of the community.

How is this community, in particular, responding to language endangerment?

They are developing immersion programs to increase the number of speakers of the language and thus ensure its preservation.

3. What different sorts of testimonies and narratives do you see in the segments of this selection?

Answers may vary, but the selection contains narratives recounting the history of how Ojibwe speakers were treated by the U.S. government, testimonials about what those experiences were like, narratives about how other groups used immersion programs to revive their languages, narratives about the experience of the immersion program, and narratives about current life in the Ojibwe community.

What roles do different kinds of speakers play as they provide information that becomes part of the program?

Answers may vary. Among the possibilities: Anton Treuer, the historian, often provides historical context that allows the audience a greater understanding of what they are watching. Louise Erdrich offers analogies that help frame how she believes the audience should think about the Ojibwe language. Eugene Stillday and Marlene Stately enter on page 632 to offer personal memories about oppression of the Ojibwe language. Brooke Ammann, Adrian Liberty, Leslie Harper, and Sean Fahrlander all provide more information about the immersion program. Larry Stillday provides descriptions that allow us to understand the Ojibwe connection to their heritage.

Is it relevant that all of the participants are Ojibwe? Why or why not?

We would argue that it's highly relevant that they are Ojibwe as it gives the participants more authority to speak about the issues facing the tribe (see next question). Among the many counterarguments one could offer is that the

**program would benefit from having non-Ojibwe partici-
pants because they might be more objective about the importance of maintaining the language.**

In what ways is their ethnicity an ethical appeal? It is important to
remember in this context that a few decades ago, there would not
have been a group of Native American scholars focusing on these
questions from an Indian perspective.

**Their ethnicity gives them the authority to speak about
what is important to their community. Their ethnicity gives
the older participants the authority to speak on the history
of the oppression of their language.**

4. The primary audience for this program is obviously not people who
   speak Ojibwe. In what ways have the program's creators accom-
   modated those of us who do not speak the language and who may
   know nothing about Ojibwe culture without overwhelming us?

   **Most obviously, they have translated most of the Ojibwe
   language in the program. Further, Anton Treuer, the historian, and Louise Erdrich, the writer, provide a great deal of
   background information to give us a context for understanding what we're reading.**

5. Writing assignment

Classroom Exercise: focus on the argument

Do you find the arguments about preventing language extinction
persuasive? To what extent should American culture or government
go to prevent language extinction? That is, how big a deal is the
threat of language extinction to those whose language is not threatened? Should English speakers be concerned about a loss of linguistic richness? Articulate several reasons in support of your opinion,
which may require researching the problem.

Michele J. Bornert *Three Blog Postings from* Deaf
Expressions   pp. 639–46

1. How would you characterize the argument made by each of
   these blog entries?

   **Answers will vary, but we would characterize the first post-
   ing as an argument of fact about the experience of deafness.
   We would characterize the second posting as a humorous**

causal argument that explores one of the effects of being deaf. We would characterize the third argument as largely a definition and proposal argument; the third posting defines ASL as a language and offers a proposal that ASL learners show patience and work hard to learn the language.

Which do you find most interesting? Most compelling? Why?

Answers will vary.

In what way does each entry present some aspect of bilingualism in the United States?

In the first post, Bornert describes a challenge brought on by being bilingual: Bornert's privacy is compromised by being bilingual because she has to reveal private medical issues to an interpreter. In the second post, Bornert uses a humorous story to illustrate how those who are bilingual have a foot in two different cultures and are sometimes excluded from one culture. In the third post, Bornert recognizes the challenge of becoming bilingual.

2. How is the bilingualism described in these entries like or unlike the bilingualism described in other selections in this chapter? What accounts for the similarities? The differences?

   Unlike other selections, these entries emphasize the aspect of choice in bilingualism; for example, the difference between "deaf" and "Deaf," her husband's desire to learn Spanish, and her role as an ASL teacher all represent the idea of choosing to be a part of two language communities. One similarity might be that all the selections emphasize the difficulties of bilingualism. Another similarity is that ASL, though not a spoken language, is a language with its own grammar and syntax, and with native speakers and language learners; that is, ASL is a language that operates as other languages do.

3. In what ways does Bornert use humor in creating her arguments?

   Possible answers: Bornert uses informal language (e.g., "deafies," "hearies," "'terps"), self-deprecating personal anecdotes (e.g., the story of not realizing her kids were playing target practice with the cat), and parenthetical comments on her writing (for example, the joke on p. 641

about not sitting around literally naked because that would be "just plain old creepy") to create humor.

How effectively does she do so?

Answers will vary.

How does her use of humor contribute to the ethos that she creates?

Answers will vary, but we would argue that Bornert displays an ability to laugh at herself that many audiences might find appealing.

4. Like most blog entries, Bornert's postings tend to be written in an informal style. What features of blogging encourage writers to be informal as they create blog entries?

Blog postings are generally short, which can give writers and readers a sense of informality. Further, because blog postings are date and time stamped and only at the top of the page, they often have a sense of being temporary because the next entry always displaces the previous posting (postings are, of course, archived, so this sense that they're temporary is deceptive).

If you visit Bornert's blog, you'll see that she also tweets. What features of tweeting shape those messages? Why?

Most obviously, tweets are strictly limited in length—only 140 characters long. The presence of hashtags helps shape those messages, too; Twitter encourages authors to enter ongoing conversations and to make that entry into a conversation obvious by using a hashtag to signal the topic of the tweet.

5. Writing assignment

Classroom Exercise: focus on the world

According to some medical experts, because of the advances in cochlear implants, being deaf is now a choice (see, for example, http://www.npr.org/2012/04/08/150245885/cochlear-implants-redefine-what-it-means-to-be-deaf). Being Deaf and identifying with the Deaf community is also a choice. What analogues could you suggest for choosing to remain deaf or for choosing to identify with the Deaf community? What are the costs and benefits of remaining deaf or of identifying with Deaf culture?

Kirk Semple *Moving to U.S. and Amassing a Fortune,*
                 No English Needed   pp. 648–51

1. What argument(s) is Semple making in this selection, specifically with regard to the necessity of immigrants to master English?

   Semple essentially argues that it's possible for immigrants to be very successful financially and socially without ever mastering English.

   What particular factors have enabled the three men who are profiled here to succeed in the United States?

   "Modern technology," "determination," and "ingenuity" are all mentioned in paragraph 15; large immigrant populations have also allowed them to function in their native languages and been interested in their products.

   What challenges have they overcome? How have they been able to do so?

   All three men faced the challenge of immigration and adapting to a new culture in addition to the challenge of not speaking the language that dominates American life. The article suggests that hard work is probably the most important way that they have been able to overcome challenges.

   How representative do you think the experiences of these three men might be? Why?

   Answers will vary.

2. How successful is Semple at constructing an argument based on fact? Use the suggestions in the "Guide to Writing an Argument of Fact" in Chapter 8 as the basis for your evaluation.

   Answers will vary. We would note that Semple probably understands his audience very well: most Americans are ready to believe arguments that suggest that hard work makes success possible even in the face of difficult obstacles.

3. Once you've completed question 2, check out the comments readers made in response to Semple's article (http://bit.ly/

ssScDQ), especially those listed as "Highlights" and those listed as "Recommendations" to see whether those posting comments would likely agree with your assessment. Do the comments you find there lead you to reassess Semple's success at creating an argument based on fact? Why or why not? (By the way, you'll notice that many of the comments refer to the Occupy Wall Street movement, which was taking place when this article was published.)

Answers will vary.

4. As you may be aware, journalists rarely get to write the titles for their articles. In fact, this article appeared with two slightly different titles, and it has been given a third title elsewhere on the *New York Times'* Web site. In the national edition of the *Times*, the article appeared with the title used here: "Moving to U.S. and Amassing a Fortune, No English Needed." The version of the article that appeared in the New York City edition was entitled "Moving to U.S. and Prospering, without English." Finally, in the "Times Topics" section of the paper's Web page that archives Semple's articles, the piece is listed as "Immigrant Entrepreneurs Succeed without English" (http://nti.ms/tYWLNh). In what sense does each title make a slightly different argument about the article that follows? Which of the titles sticks most closely to the facts? Which might be said to contain additional emotional appeals? (See Chapter 2 for a discussion of arguments based on emotions.)

Answers may vary. We would argue that "Immigrant Entrepreneurs Succeed without English" sticks most closely to the facts. "Moving to the U.S. and Amassing a Fortune, No English Needed" seems to make the most emotional appeals. The use of the words "amassing a fortune" seems to us much more loaded than the idea of "prospering." "No English Needed" seems more dismissive of the importance of learning English than does the relatively reserved phrase "without English." The former makes it seem as though the entrepreneurs rejected the idea of learning English, while the latter seems to suggest that they were able to run successful businesses without learning the language but not necessarily while rejecting the idea.

5. Writing assignment

Do non-English speakers in America have an obligation to learn English? Do English speakers have an obligation to teach them? Under what circumstances do you feel that the federal or state government should make English classes available to non-English-speaking immigrants? What responsibility do non-English-speaking immigrants have to learn the language on their own? In an ideal world, what do you think the official policy of your state (or the whole country) should be?

Amy Martinez Starke *Hmong Elder Didn't Forget*
the Old Ways   pp. 653–55

1. How is Sao Yee Cha's bilingualism like and unlike that of others whose experiences have been described in this chapter?

   Most of the others in this chapter (Cisneros, Tan, Cao, Dumas, and Agosín) are all fluent in at least two languages and highly literate in English; all learned English at a younger age and are fluent in English, even, with the exception of Agosín, choosing it as the primary language in which they write. Like Sao Yee Cha, though, all have felt separated from the mainstream English-speaking culture that has surrounded them.

2. What sort of occasion gives rise to an obituary—forensic, deliberative, or epideictic? (The answer may be more complex than it seems. For a discussion of occasions for argument, see Chapter 1.)

   Obituaries are most commonly epideictic or ceremonial arguments, but they could easily be forensic arguments that attempt to make sense of what happened in the past. They're unlikely to be deliberative, though it's not impossible, as a speaker might want to use the example of someone else's life as a spur to pursue a future action.

3. In what ways do the illustrations that accompany this selection form part of the argument? What do they contribute to the force of the argument? (For a discussion of visual arguments, see Chapter 14.)

   Answers will vary, but may include how the images highlight, especially in the clothing and the surroundings,

the vast differences between the two cultures Sao Yee Cha lived in.

4–5. Writing assignments

Classroom Exercise: focus on the world

Obituaries are commonly epideictic arguments; that is, they seek to praise or blame someone for their character or accomplishments or lack thereof. Try your hand at crafting an epideictic text—praise or blame a person, place, or thing. To add some extra interest to your piece, consider working against the conventional wisdom about your subject—praise someone or something we might ordinarily think of as deserving blame, or blame someone or something we normally praise.

Wrap-up Exercises for "What's It Like to Be Bilingual in the United States?"

These assignments are suggested as wrap-up exercises in which students can integrate any or all of the readings of the chapter. Either would be suitable for an in-class essay assignment.

1. Write an essay in which you take to task the writer whose argument you find least convincing among those you read in this chapter. In other words, critique that writer's argument, demonstrating why your perspective on the topic is better supported. One of your tasks as a writer will be to summarize the argument you're critiquing so that readers unfamiliar with the original text will understand both the original writer's position and yours.

2. Write an argument about language(s) and identities in which you incorporate your own experiences as a user of the language varieties you know (or those you do not know). How, for example, do you imagine your life might be different if you knew certain languages or certain varieties of English, or how would it be different if you did not know the language(s) or varieties that you do? How would the command of these linguistic varieties shape your identity as an individual or as a member of the groups to which you belong?

   Another way of imagining this assignment, if you are monolingual, is to think about what your life would have been like if you'd grown up in a community where a language other than

English was used (perhaps exclusively, perhaps in addition to English). What challenges might you have faced thus far with respect to mastering the language(s) of your home community? Those used outside the home community? How might dealing with these challenges have influenced the way you perceive yourself both inside and outside the community? Similarly, if you grew up bilingually, imagine what your life would be like if you were monolingual. How would you be different?

CHAPTER 24

Why Worry about Food and Water?

Everyone eats, and the readings in this chapter reflect a belief that this activity of consuming that takes up so much of our time and energy deserves more careful consideration. The readings encourage students to think more seriously not only about the food that they choose to eat but also about how food choices fit into larger patterns of culture and consumption. Though food has become a popular topic of debate, and though Americans seem to be thinking more about their food and its origins than they did before, students probably still come to our classes without thinking of food as a major issue for debate. This chapter therefore gives them rich opportunities to explore an area they know quite a lot about but which may not have been framed for them in the ways that these readings do. Some of the questions that the chapter encourages us to ask include the following:

- Beyond satisfying our hunger and thirst, what should we think about when we think about food and water?
- What responsibilities to our communities and to the environment do our food choices reflect?
- How do we even understand what it means to eat and drink responsibly in a world where much of what we consume comes through corporate intermediaries?

Mark Bittman *Is Junk Food Really Cheaper?*   pp. 660–64

1. What is Bittman's argument?

    Bittman argues that cooking real food is good for our financial, physical, and cultural health.

    How would you characterize it? Is it an argument of fact? Of definition? Of evaluation? A causal argument? A proposal?

    We would suggest that this piece is, ultimately, a proposal argument that we should make cooking a priority.

However you characterize it, find examples of the other kinds of argument in Bittman's argument as well.

A few possibilities:

Argument of fact: see paragraph 8 ("The fact is that most people can afford real food.")

Argument of definition: see paragraphs 13 and 14, where Bittman argues that fast food is an addictive drug

Argument of evaluation: see paragraphs 5 and 6, where he argues that food cooked at home is better than other options

Causal argument: see paragraph 13 for a causal argument about how fast food acts like a drug

2. Interestingly, Bittman admits that "rational arguments only go so far" (paragraph 12), a major assumption of this textbook. By this point in the selection, what rational arguments has Bittman presented for his claims?

Bittman's comparison of costs is a rational argument; the argument in paragraph 4 that we should not measure a food's value by calorie count alone is a rational argument; paragraph 6 provides a rational argument about the alternatives to junk food; paragraphs 8 and 9 contain rational arguments about Americans' proximity to supermarkets.

Following this concession, what arguments does he offer in discussing why rational arguments are insufficient to change the situation he is criticizing?

Bittman argues that powerful marketing sways us and processed food has created a food carnival that has created addictions to processed food, addictions that cannot be overcome by rational argument.

3. What sort of ethos does Bittman create for himself in this essay? Based on this article, what sort of person do you think he might be? Why?

Answers will vary. Some readers might suggest that Bittman is concerned about public health and committed to finding solutions. Others might find him condescending and

impractical. However students respond, ask them to locate specific textual evidence that leads them to draw the conclusions that they reach.

4. Study the visual feature carefully. How is it designed to make an argument?

The numbers in the feature make the relatively high costs of the fast food especially prominent, and the inset graphics highlight the differences in nutritional value. Further, the pictures of the fast food feature the food in packaging, reinforcing the idea that it is artificial, while the other pictures emphasize a more wholesome, natural appearance of the nonprocessed food.

How does it contribute support to Bittman's article?

The visual reinforces the difference in cost by labeling the cost of every ingredient in the pictures of the unprocessed (or less processed) food.

What design features make it especially effective?

Answers will vary.

5. As Chapter 7 explains, effective writers qualify their claims in order to represent the complexity of reality, on the one hand, and in order to make their task simpler, on the other—after all, it is generally much easier to provide sufficient support for a qualified claim than for one that is not qualified in some way. How does Bittman qualify his claims? Make a list of places in the article where he qualifies a claim and/or acknowledges a counterargument before seeking to demonstrate that his perspective is the better one.

Answers will vary. Among the possibilities: Paragraph 1 is a counterargument that Bittman will attack in his second paragraph. The first sentence of paragraph 4 is a counterargument that Bittman introduces before his own argument. In the first sentence of paragraph 10, Bittman qualifies his argument when he acknowledges that "[t]aking the long route to putting food on the table may not be easy, but for almost all Americans it remains a choice." He also introduces qualifications in paragraph 12, when he writes, "[t]he

**ubiquity, convenience, and habit-forming appeal of hyper-
processed foods have largely drowned out the alternatives"
because he is again noting the difficulty of adopting his solution of more cooking at home. In paragraph 19, Bittman
considers how to change a culture and notes that "[t]he answers, not surprisingly, are complex," which qualifies his
argument by noting that the changes he calls for are difficult to effect.**

6. Writing assignment

Classroom Exercise: focus on the world

Part of Bittman's ethos comes from his relative fame as a columnist for
the *New York Times* and as a host of his own cooking show. Ask students to view one or more cooking shows on television or to think
more carefully about cooking shows that they have seen. In what ways
does celebrity affect the show and the food that the hosts prepare?
How does the host talk about food? What values about food does the
show seem to hold and promote? In class, have students talk about
how different hosts approach food so that the class can understand
what it means to have different approaches to and values about food.

Wikipedia *Local Food* and *Farm-to-Table*   pp. 666–77

1. In what ways is an encyclopedia entry, including one in a collaborative, online reference work like Wikipedia, an argument? What
   kind of argument is it or should it be? What evidence can you cite
   for your claims?

   **Encyclopedia articles are generally arguments to inform an
   audience. In this case, the entry is largely a definition argument, laying out the criteria for which food may be considered "local food."**

2. The audiences for encyclopedia entries are always multiple. On
   the one hand, people with no background in a given subject
   should be able to read an entry and get a clear picture of the state
   of knowledge on that subject, including current debates about it.
   On the other hand, experts on a topic should be able to read an
   entry, nodding approvingly as they move through the article and
   finding that the relevant information has been presented clearly
   and faithfully. Did you find that the creators of this article wrote

appropriately for someone with your level of knowledge on the subject? Why or why not? How does your response compare to those of your classmates, who may have read the articles with different amounts or kinds of background knowledge?

Answers will vary.

3. An interesting part of Wikipedia is the way in which it makes the collaborative process visible to those who wish to participate in it or understand it. For example, at the top of the entries, readers often see tabs labeled "Article," "Discussion" or "Read" (which discuss aspects of the entry), "Edit" (which permits authorized users to post editorial changes), and "View History" (which keep track of all changes made and the person making them). As the notes at the beginning of each of these entries indicate, there was a suggestion that the second entry be merged into the first, a suggestion that was ultimately rejected. To what extent do you see the two entries as overlapping? To what extent do you see them as different? Should they be merged? (You may want to consult the "Discussion" on these entries; if the archive on this discussion is still available, it may give you some additional ideas about the links between the two entries.)

   Answers will vary; see response to question 4 for more ideas about discussing this article.

4–5. Writing assignments

Classroom Exercise: focus on rhetoric

You can teach students a great deal about how knowledge is constructed in Wikipedia by having them contribute to articles. First, give them some time in class to brainstorm things that they know a lot about, whatever that subject may be. Next, have them read Wikipedia articles on the subjects of their expertise to look for holes— where could they add useful information or an external link that would provide background? Once they've discovered places where they can add information, have them edit articles. Students who do not have them will need to create wiki accounts and send you their usernames so that you can track their edits. Not only will students who contribute to a Wikipedia article have a deeper understanding of how knowledge is constructed there, but they are also likely to be more sensitive to the importance of evaluating sources carefully.

Making a Visual Argument: Apples to Oranges

Claire Ironside *Apples to Oranges*   pp. 679–89

1. What is Ironside's explicit argument?

   Her explicit argument is that food brought in from a distance requires more fossil-fuel consumption than food grown more locally.

   What kind of argument is it (for example, of fact or definition)?

   An argument of fact that is meant to inform.

   Might she be making an implicit argument? What would that argument be? And what kind of argument is it?

   She might be making an implicit proposal argument that we should choose local food.

2. Analyze each pair of pages in Ironside's argument. What does each juxtaposition contribute to her argument?

   The first two pages introduce us to the idea of comparing apples and oranges (an ironic choice given that the phrase "apples and oranges" is usually meant to describe things that shouldn't be compared). The second two pages offer us a graphic representation and a verbal explanation of how many fossil-fuel calories we expend on average for each food calorie we consume, thus giving us a context where we might hope to be able to reduce the input of fossil fuels. The third pair of images dramatically illustrates the difference in distance traveled for a local apple versus a California orange, making it somewhat more concrete than if we had only heard the difference stated in numbers. The fourth image allows us to see the difference in how the fossil-fuel inputs contribute to the delivery of the food and where the energy goes (reactions will vary, but we wonder if this image might not confuse some readers, since the previous image makes a much more clear-cut argument). The final image illustrates the overall difference in fossil-fuel consumption for each piece of fruit compared to average.

   How would you characterize the purpose of the comparison related to fossil-fuel inputs?

This graphic is an argument to inform that teaches us that all food that we buy (and almost all food that we grow) requires some investment of fossil fuels, but it also tells us the differences in how those fossil-fuel inputs are allocated.

What value might there be in the details given?

Answers may vary, but we tend to think that this juxtaposition reminds us that almost all food requires fossil-fuel inputs, but that we might want those inputs to be more for things like cooking and preparation than for trucking across long distances.

What sorts of conclusions might we draw from this juxtaposition?

Answers may vary, but we lean toward a conclusion that local food generally contributes to a cleaner environment and a more sensible allocation of fossil-fuel energy.

3. Evaluate the visual aspects of Ironside's argument, including her choice of colors.

   Answers will vary.

4. Writing assignment
5. Visual argument or writing assignment

Classroom Exercise: focus on the argument

As question 1 suggests, Ironside is likely making an implicit argument that we should eat more local food. You might ask students to detail what they ate at their last meal and try to figure out where their food came from—are they eating locally? Do they even know how to find out? You might also ask them to think about what it would mean to eat locally all the time. Would they be willing to eat produce only in season? Are there foods that must be imported that they would never give up? Are there good arguments for not worrying about eating locally?

Eric Mortenson *A Diversified Farm Prospers in Oregon's Willamette Valley by Going Organic and Staying Local* pp. 691–93

1. What arguments is Mortenson making in this article?

   Mortenson argues that small, diversified organic farms can be successful even though they face daunting challenges.

He also argues that successful farming should be measured by other means than profit alone.

In what ways does the information here help you understand the challenges of being an independent farmer in the United States at this historical moment?

Some possibilities: The information makes clear the financial challenges of independent farming, the importance of factors outside one's control such as the weather, and the sheer hard work that running a small farm entails.

In what ways does it give you useful information about the relationships many Americans have with the food they consume?

Answers will vary. For many audiences, an article like this might highlight how little many Americans know about where their food comes from, while for some audiences it might be yet another article romanticizing organic farms.

2. What sorts of hard evidence does Mortenson use in this selection?

   Mortenson includes, in paragraphs 15 through 23, hard evidence about how the Boyers make money, including exact figures on how much the Boyers earn from their conservation project on the river and Barbara Boyer's job at the farmer's market. He includes exact figures to offer evidence for how much work the Boyers do (see paragraphs 16 and 17 for this evidence). He also uses extensive testimony from the Boyers themselves.

   How effectively does he use them?

   Answers will vary.

3. As is often the case in such newspaper articles, Mortenson seeks to create the Boyers as three-dimensional characters by describing them in some detail. Watch the video posted with this article. In what ways has Mortenson captured aspects of each of the Boyers' personality?

   Answers will vary, but some possibilities include that Mortenson has effectively described Barbara Boyer's energy and gregariousness and Tom Boyer's quietness.

Are there other details he might have added? How do such details serve as arguments based on emotion, ethos, or fact?

Details about the Boyers can be said to be based on emotion when they encourage us to identify with the couple or find them sympathetic (for example, in paragraphs 26–28 when the Mortenson highlights Boyer's commitment to the idea of heritage). The details can serve as arguments based on ethos when they're included to make us trust the Boyers and see them as ethically or morally good people (for example, the detail in paragraph 40 that the Boyers have only worked two Sundays in the past 18 years) or when the details are meant to make us appreciate the Boyers' accomplishments (for example, paragraph 8, when Tom Boyer's intellectual habits are mentioned). The details are arguments based on fact when they establish the origins of the Boyers (for example, in paragraph 10, when we learn of Barbara Boyer's background).

4. This article has received two posted comments, which are reproduced here as written:

ecohumanist October 02, 2011 at 8:48AM

> I am really glad that this far in the willamette valley stayed local. It would be sad to see another farm move to mexico or china.
>
> It's time to have a serious discussion about sustainability. These "local" and "organic" farms that cater to wealthy limousine liberals are NOT PART OF A GLOBAL SOLUTION!

ruonboard October 02, 2011 at 8:59AM

> Great story. These people are enjoying success and happiness through a positive use of their land. The bonus is the fact that their efforts also help others in the community. This is a great example of the benefits of doing things right and free market capitalism. Kudos.

Even though Portland has a reputation of being an especially liberal city, neither of these comments is especially liberal in its stance. The first criticizes "wealthy limousine liberals," just the sort of folks who are often seen as supporting the local food or farm-to-table movement described in the Wikipedia entries in an earlier selection while the second interprets the

Boyers' actions as evidence of what happens when "free market capitalism" is allowed to work. On the other hand, we can imagine many liberal supports of the local food movement (not just "wealthy limousine liberal" folk) who find much to like in the article as well. What does this situation remind us about the complexities of audience?

One possibility is that people can use different reasoning to arrive at the same conclusion; another possibility is that any audience can take almost any piece of evidence to support what they already thought about at an issue.

5. Writing assignment

Classroom Exercise: focus on the world

As this article implies but never quite states, at the heart of many ethical arguments about food is the role of large corporations in food production. As a class, research the issue of how agribusiness affects food. A good starting point is Culinate.com's collection of ten Web sites about sustainable food, available at http://www.culinate.com/articles/features/sustainable_food_resouces_online, but you should also encourage students to seek out defenses of industrial agriculture, such as farmer Blake Hurst's article from the magazine of the American Enterprise Institute, available at http://www.american.com/archive/2009/july/the-omnivore2019s-delusion-against-the-agri-intellectuals. Use the information that the students gather to stage a debate in class.

Adriene Hill *Eating Ethically—It's Complicated [and Listener Comments]* pp. 696–701

1. What was your response to Hill's audio feature before you read the comments? After you read them?

Answers will vary.

2. As noted, the focus of *Marketplace* is business and the economy. Hence, we can assume that listeners to the program share those interests or are interested in learning about those perspectives on the news of the day. How do we see those concerns reflected in the comments posted about this feature?

Many of the commenters argued along economic lines. For example, Thomas Wallace, the first commenter, argues that

buying locally benefits the local economy by keeping money in that local economy. Or consider the comment from Pat Krueger, who argues that the primary consideration in choosing whether to eat meat and dairy should be the need for those in the meat and dairy industries to make a living. (Ask students to consider alternatives: the audience for another show might emphasize the environmental effects of food choices, while another audience might focus on the taste of food.)

3. Which part or parts of Hill's features did those commenting find most problematic?

The most problematic part of the feature seems to be the claim that eating locally can negatively affect small farmers in other countries.

From the perspective of Toulmin, Hill and one of the experts she interviewed seem to have assumed a warrant that was not shared by listeners who posted comments on this topic. How could this warrant be stated?

Hill and the experts suggest that we should consider the economic status of all small farmers equally; many of the commenters, on the other hand, believe that Americans should focus primarily on the economic status of American farmers.

Might Hill have prepared her listeners in some way for the information that was presented in this section of the feature by making the warrant explicit or qualifying the claims made?

Answers may vary, but Hill might have been more explicit about what she means by ethical eating and ethical choices. In other words, she might be more specific about to whom she believes we are responsible when we make food choices.

4. Are all the criticisms of Hill's feature valid? (In other words, should you trust a commenter any more than you trust Hill?)

As the title of this book suggests, all of the commenters are making arguments—their claims are not necessarily more trustworthy than Hill's, and *perhaps* slightly less so since they are not subject to an editor as Hill's story is.

For example, investigate Thomas Wallace's claim about whether most local food is grown seasonally outside. Is this claim valid anywhere in the United States? Everywhere? A trip to the grocery store might give you some idea about whether it is, although you'll likely need to do a bit more research to determine the extent to which this claim is valid. And what of his argument about tomatoes grown in hothouses? After all, it may be true that wood waste could be used to heat hothouses, but what is the likelihood that it is or will be?

Wallace's claim that most food grown locally is grown outside may be valid if we consider that he's likely writing about food grown for farmer's markets and other small outlets. Our research suggests that using wood waste to heat hothouses remains more the exception than the rule.

5. Writing assignment

Classroom Exercise: focus on the argument

At the end of Hill's report, she recommends that those who want to eat ethically should "eat less meat" and then adds, "I feel like I always wind up saying that." One of the most frequently debated issues in food ethics is the ethics of eating meet. Ask students if they find arguments about ethical vegetarianism persuasive. Do they find such arguments persuasive? If so, why? If not, why not? What do they think are the best arguments for vegetarianism? What are the best arguments against a vegetarian diet? Are there any pro-vegetarian arguments that they think their peers would find especially persuasive?

Christophe Pelletier   *The Locavore's Dilemma*   pp. 703–6

1. What is Pelletier's argument?

Pelletier argues that eating locally is not a practical solution for food and farming.

How well does he support it?

Answers will vary, but when discussing responses to this question in class, press students to identify specific rhetorical moves or pieces of evidence that they find particularly effective or ineffective.

How is it similar to yet different from Hill's argument in the previous selection, "Eating Ethically—It's Complicated"?

Both arguments recognize that "eating locally" is not a simple solution but instead is an approach that can have negative consequences in addition to positive effects. However, Hill's argument treats eating locally more seriously as an ethical choice; Pelletier is far more dismissive of the concept as hypocritical and backwards looking.

What, for Pelletier, is the problem with the notion of eating locally?

The notion of eating locally is unrealistic for most people and ignores the progress that trade creates in the world. Further, he contends that "the idea quickly evolves into an ideology" that leads to impractical decisions.

Do you think he is concerned about the ethics of our eating patterns?

We would suggest that Pelletier is concerned about the ethics of our eating patterns and cite the beginning of paragraph 6, where he argues that we should emphasize "efficient and low environmental impact" farming and eating practices. However, we would also suggest that the ethics of eating patterns are only part of Pelletier's concern: his argument emphasizes economics and the pleasures of eating varied foods in addition to ethical concerns.

2. We expect proposal arguments to have an evaluative component. What specifically does Pelletier evaluate and critique?

Pelletier evaluates claims made by locavores about the value of their food choices.

What criteria does he use for making his evaluative claims?

His criteria include the honesty of the claims, how effectively those who make them follow their own ideas, the logical consistency of the claims (that is, if we should eat locally, should we buy everything locally?), and the actual environmental impact of food miles.

3. In the closing paragraphs of the blog posting, Pelletier offers a proposal: his predictions about local production and local markets in the future. What specific predictions does he make?

Pelletier predicts that urban farming will become a more significant part of the urban experience and that perishable commodities will be produced in and close to cities while nonperishable commodities will continue to be raised in the same locations but with improved transportation networks that will get them to urban consumers more quickly and efficiently.

How well do you think he has supported them?

Answers will vary.

How do you think the experts quoted in Hill's radio feature and those posting comments on that feature might respond to Pelletier's predictions? Why?

Answers may vary, though we think that many of the experts and commenters in Hill's piece would approve of Pelletier's practical approach to the economics of food and his recognition of the complexity of the issues involved.

4. What sort of ethos does Pelletier create for himself?

We would suggest that Pelletier creates an ethos as a bit of a contrarian, or someone who likes to go against current popular opinion, though toward the end he takes on more of an ethos of someone who sees the long view; that is, he presents himself as someone who understands a long arc of history and who can therefore make predictions about the future.

Do you think he is someone you would like? Why or why not? In particular, how do you respond to his use of humor—at least mild sarcasm—in the opening paragraphs of this blog posting when he is criticizing British Columbians who love coffee, beer, chocolate, and other foodstuffs, on the one hand, but might claim to be committed locavores, on the other? Is this an effective way of making these arguments?

Answers will vary.

5. Writing assignment

Classroom Exercise: focus on the argument

In June 2012 Pierre Desrochers and Hiroko Shimizu published *The Locavore's Dilemma: In Praise of the 10,000-Mile Diet*. You can read an excerpt from the book at http://www.salon.com/ 2012/06/16/eating_local_hurts_the_planet/. Of course, the locavore idea is hotly debated, and students can easily find more sources on both sides of the issue. What ideas about being a locavore—or about not being a locavore—do they find most persuasive? Why? How difficult would it be to be a locavore in the area where your school is located? You might ask students to visit a local farmer's market and interview the farmers who sell there to gain more perspective on the issue.

Malia Wollan *Migration, on Ice: How Globalization Kills Chickens for Their Parts*   pp. 708–12

1. What sort of response do you have to Wollan's essay? What is your rational response—the response that focuses on facts and reason? What sort of affective or emotional response do you have? If you eat chicken—and truth be told, similar stories can likely be told not only about other kinds of meat but about many other foods as well—what sort of response did you find yourself having as you read the selection?

Answers will vary.

2. How would you characterize Wollan's argument? Is it an argument of fact? Of definition? Of evaluation? A causal argument? A proposal? What evidence can you give for your claim?

Overall, we would characterize this as an argument of fact. We would highlight two sentences as evidence that the overall argument is one of fact: "In this globalized market, a woman eating a salad at a Wendy's in Maine could be ingesting the breast of the same chicken whose gizzard flavors a chicken stew in Togo and whose thigh is served with borscht in Moscow and whose excess fat will soon go to a Conoco Phillips refinery in Texas to make synthetic diesel fuel" and "In Ghana, it is cheaper to buy frozen Tyson chicken parts shipped across the Atlantic Ocean in temperature-controlled cargo containers than it is to buy a freshly slaughtered chicken from the neighbor down the street" (paragraphs 8 and 9). In these sentences we see how Wollan uses statements

of surprising fact to establish a global market for chicken parts that most readers probably did not know existed.

Once you've decided which of these kinds of arguments best characterizes the selection as a whole, look for sections of the article that represent other kinds of arguments.

Answers will vary. We offer two possibilities below.

Definition argument: paragraphs 4 and 6 offer definition arguments based on countries' affinities for different types of chicken

Causal argument: in paragraph 12 William Awuku Ahiadormey offers a causal argument explaining why Ghanaian poultry producers have difficulty competing with American poultry producers

3. The headnote explains that *Meatpaper*, the magazine where this article first appeared, assumes that meat is "polarizing"—"divisive and universal, delicious and disturbing, funny and dead-serious"—and it seeks to understand its subject in all its complexity. How well did Wollan's article succeed in helping the magazine reach its goal? Why and how?

   Answers will vary, though we would suggest that Wollan's article succeeds because it introduces dilemmas without suggesting that there are easy answers (see paragraph 19, for example, where she notes that "cheap protein is both a blessing and a curse").

4. To what extent does the information presented in this selection (and perhaps in some of the earlier readings) provide evidence for the claim that the local food movement is the concern of "wealthy limousine liberals" and those who generally do not have to struggle to survive, whether we think about issues of social class in this country or the global situation more broadly? As you'll recall, "wealthy limousine liberals" is a phrase that occurs in a comment posted in response to Mortenson's feature on the Boyers, "A Diversified Farm Prospers in Oregon's Willamette Valley by Going Organic and Staying Local," earlier in this chapter.

   Answers will vary. This selection offers evidence that local food could be of great concern to those who have to struggle to survive. For example, what if the imported chicken really

did put poultry production in Ghana out of business? And then what if Tyson could make more money shipping chicken to a country other than Ghana? How quickly could the Ghanaian poultry industry rebound? How much damage could reliance on imported food do to the Ghanaian population and economy? On the other hand, this article could be evidence that being part of a global economy and supply system is the best option because it provides low-cost nutrition and provides the food that people actually enjoy eating.

5. Writing assignment

Classroom Exercise: focus on the world

Ask students to think of their own food traditions and what role food plays in their cultural traditions. How do these traditions interact with the culture around them? Do their traditions help them feel a sense of belonging? Do they make them feel isolated from others? Can they articulate any ways that their own traditions affect the world food supply or other food issues outside their own immediate sphere?

Mark Coleman *Review of* Bottlemania: How Water Went on Sale and Why We Bought It   pp. 714–15

1. How would you characterize Mark Coleman's evaluation of Elizabeth Royte's book? Do you think that he likes the book? How well? Why? What evidence can you cite for your characterization of his evaluation?

   Overall, Coleman seems to like the book. He praises it as "tautly paced" and admires her "mordant wit" and "intellectual curiosity." Students should be able to find ample evidence of his approval of the book.

2. A review of a book (or movie or DVD or concert) is, by definition, an evaluative argument. What criteria does Coleman use in evaluating Royte's book? Do these criteria seem appropriate and sufficient to the task? Why or why not? (For a discussion of evaluative arguments, see Chapter 10.)

   Answers will vary, but some possibilities for criteria include intellectual complexity; writing that is well paced; entertainment value; and pragmatism in approach to issues surrounding bottled water.

3. Coleman contends that as a writer, "Royte doesn't traffic in platitudes, moral certainties or oversimplification; she's unafraid of
   ambiguity" (paragraph 2). What evidence do you find for these
   claims in his review? Should you find any?

   **Answers will vary. One possibility: Coleman notes that
   Royte mentions the appeal that bottled water holds even
   though for the most part she finds it objectionable.**

4. Examine Coleman's use of quotations from Royte's book. What
   functions do they serve in Coleman's own argument? (In answering this question, you may wish to make a list of all the quotations to examine their functions carefully.)

   **Answers will vary. Some possibilities include that they il-
   lustrate points that he makes about the quality of her writing (such as the idea that she knows how to get out of the
   way) while other quotations help persuade the audience
   that issues surrounding bottled water are important enough
   to be taken seriously.**

5. Writing assignment

Classroom Exercise: focus on rhetoric

Many book reviews and some movie reviews do not seem to be
straightforward evaluations; they don't end with recommendations
to read or not to read or to view or not to view. Instead, these reviews provide an overview of the argument of the book under discussion and often contribute their own knowledge on the topic. Ask
your students to try their hand at such a review. They can review a
book or film (or other media production) and write an evaluation
that works to understand meaning and significance as well as judge
the quality of the product under review.

Elizabeth Royte *Excerpt from* Bottlemania: How
Water Went on Sale and Why
We Bought It   pp. 717–24

1. Briefly summarize Royte's response to the question with which
   she begins this excerpt.

   **Royte suggests that, unless we have strong reasons for con-
   cern about our water or our reactions to potential patho-**

gens, we should probably drink our tap water; ideally, though, we should install point-of-use filters.

How well does she support her conclusions?

Answers will vary.

2. Summarize the arguments that are made by the *New York Times* graphic on pp. 723–24, and describe several contexts in which it could conceivably be used.

   The graphic argues that Americans consume huge quantities of bottled water, suggesting also that they are drinking less tap water. The graphic about rates of consumption could be used in marketing or in public health contexts or if a store were trying to decide what products to stock. The bottled water consumption graph might contribute to discussions about plastic recycling or solid waste handling or in marketing decisions for beverage companies.

   Evaluate the graphic's effectiveness as a visual argument. (You may wish to locate the *Times* article with which this graphic originally appeared and use that information as part of your evaluation. For a discussion of evaluative arguments, see Chapter 10. For a discussion of visual arguments, see Chapter 14.)

   Answers will vary.

3. In paragraph 2 of the previous selection, Mark Coleman's review of Royte's book, Coleman claims that "Royte doesn't traffic in platitudes, moral certainties or oversimplification; she's unafraid of ambiguity." What evidence for his evaluation do you see in this excerpt from Royte's book?

   Answers will vary, but we suggest one sentence as a good piece of evidence: "Certainly, nearly everything humans do has an environmental impact—biking to work, recycling newspapers, and drinking tap water included." That sentence provides a good example of her tolerance of ambiguity since all of these activities are generally thought of as environmentally responsible.

4. One of the ways that readers know that Royte is writing for a popular audience rather than an academic one is that she does

not use footnotes or precise references (for example, page numbers) or quotations. She includes a list of works entitled "Selected Bibliography and Further Reading" at the end of the book, although it is not comprehensive, as we discovered tracking down the references for the three works that she cited in this excerpt (which we have presented as a Works Cited list). What are the advantages and disadvantages of using footnotes and explicit citations from a writer's point of view? A reader's? A publisher's?

Answers will vary, but we suggest a few possibilities. Leaving out explicit citations is better for writers and publishers in that they don't require extreme precision or require extra pages (which can be costly); readers might appreciate the uncluttered text and the list of resources that they might actually consult rather than an intimidating list of sources. The inclusion of footnotes, however, can build the ethos of both author and publisher, and footnotes allow readers to track down exact sources of information.

How does the absence of footnotes and explicit citations influence your evaluation of her text? Does it make it less formal and more inviting? Does it weaken Royte's ethos as a credible, trustworthy author? Why?

Answers will vary.

5. Writing assignment

Classroom Exercise: focus on the world

Count how many bottles of water, disposable or reusable, are in your classroom on the day that you discuss this piece. Also count how many are in your office, car, or home and share that with the class, and ask your students to do the same. To what degree does the presence of bottled water simply represent part of American consumerism? (You might, for example, ask students to count something else in their homes—how many spoons or sweaters do they have? Do they really need them all?) Is bottled water something that they have good reasons to buy? Ask them to write a short evaluative essay defending bottled water.

Cook's Country Magazine *Ready-to-Bake Chocolate Chip Cookies* pp. 726–27

Cook's Illustrated Magazine *Solving the Mystery of the Chewy Chocolate Chip Cookie* pp. 728–30

1. What kind of argument is the first section of "Ready-to-Bake Chocolate Chip Cookies"? (For example, an argument of fact or of definition?) The list of recommended products?

   Both sections are heavily evaluative, but they also contain some causal arguments (e.g., adding more chips will make homemade cookies better), and the suggestion that one can bake better cookies cheaper and without preservatives could be read as a proposal argument.

   What kind of argument is "Solving the Mystery of the Chewy Chocolate Chip Cookie"? The recipe? What evidence can you provide for your claims?

   "Solving the Mystery" is largely a definition argument in which the authors establish the criteria for a certain type of cookie that they want to produce. "The Solution" section of the article is mostly a causal argument. The recipe itself might be seen as a proposal argument or perhaps a causal argument.

2. Examine carefully the first section of "Ready-to-Bake Chocolate Chip Cookies" and the first section of "Thick and Chewy Chocolate Chip Cookies." What sorts of ethical appeals do you find in each?

   Possibilities: the authors' description of their scientific rigor or the citation of Shirley Corriher, a food scientist, as a source.

   What sorts of emotional appeals do you find?

   Possibilities: the authors' references to saving money and avoiding artificial ingredients might be considered emotional appeals, as they're focusing on values that the audience holds.

To facts and reason? (For a discussion of kinds of appeals, see Chapters 2, 3, and 4.)

Possibilities: the scientific explanation of what makes good cookies or the precise instructions in the recipes.

3–4. **Answers will vary, as will the quality of any cookies the students might bake. But you should still require them to share some cookies with you, explaining that it strengthens their ethos. (Overall, *Cook's Illustrated* generally targets serious home cooks who are interested in challenging recipes and precise instructions. *Cook's Country* targets home cooks who prefer more traditional food, and though some of their recipes can be challenging, this magazine often emphasizes quicker and easier recipes than does *Cook's Illustrated*.)**

5. Writing assignment

Classroom Exercise: focus on rhetoric

Given that there's no accounting for personal tastes, how do we make arguments about food and drink? Whose authority do you trust when it comes to judging the quality of food? What knowledge, skills, experience, or charisma makes someone trustworthy on the issue of what makes food good? Are there considerations beyond a good palate? Is it worth it to try to "educate" one's palate to learn to appreciate a wider variety of foods and flavors? Are acquired tastes worth acquiring? Why or why not?

Wrap-up Exercises for "Why Worry about Food and Water?"

1. Claire Ironside's visual argument "Apples to Oranges" encourages us to think about food and its environmental impact; Adriene Hill and Christophe Pelletier focus on how to define ethical eating; the *Cook's Illustrated* recipe for chocolate chip cookies emphasizes aesthetic appeals, including taste, to the exclusion of almost everything else. Using a Rogerian approach, write an essay in which you argue for a particular approach to thinking about how we should eat. For example, should we think most about food as a social experience, or about calorie count, cost, ease of acquisition, or nutritional value (however you define "nutritional value")? You might try experimenting with making an argument

that you don't feel entirely convinced is true just to gain practice thinking about how to use evidence. Be sure to make it clear who your intended audience is.

2. Record everything that you eat and drink for one, two, or three days; then write an essay that explores some aspect of your consumption. For example, you could write about how much food you consumed that you or someone you know prepared versus how much you ate that was prepared in restaurants or factories. You could examine the distance traveled by the foods you ate, as far as you can determine. Perhaps recording what food you eat will encourage you to begin an experiment, such as trying to eat all local food, all vegan food, or all fast food—in short, you might try eating differently from your normal routine. Prepare an essay about your experience of paying more attention than usual to what you eat and drink.

3. Choose one reading from this chapter that you think makes the best case for teaching us how to think about food and water, and choose a few readings that you think do not provide as strong a case for how we should think about food. Write an evaluation argument for why the reading you chose presents the strongest case, and be careful to articulate your criteria clearly.

CHAPTER 25

What Should "Diversity on Campus" Mean and Why?

Because Americans believe that all people are equal, our colleges and universities strive to include students of diverse backgrounds to ensure that one group of people is not dominating the educated class. Equally important, schools seek diversity to enrich the learning environment by bringing a multiplicity of voices and experiences to campus. But what if certain ideologies take hold of academia? What if we have been misreading the effects of diversity or have an overly limited understanding of what constitutes diversity? And how real is purposeful, calculated diversity? The readings in this cluster invite us to consider what problems need to be fixed and what actions should be taken to fix them. This consideration leads us to ask the following questions:

- What constitutes true diversity? How do we measure diversity? What determining characteristics of identity allow us to measure diversity?
- Should educational institutions be representative of the city, state, or U.S. population in race? Gender? Political ideology? Religion? Sexual orientation? What characteristics are the most important to balance? Why?
- Schools still talk about diversity and affirmative action, but there is a large movement to remove any preferential admission or hiring programs for minorities of any type. What are the disadvantages of these programs? What alternatives are there to affirmative action programs?

Making a Visual Argument: Student-Designed Diversity Posters

Joseph Wagner *Peeling Off Labels*

Anthony Jackson *Through Our Identities We Create a Community of Diversity*

Bailey Jones *Speak Out about Diversity*

Stephanie Heyman *Everyone a Part, No One Apart*

Melanie Frost *Embracing Diversity in University Residences*

Hannah Leimback *Identities Are Infinite . . . What's Yours?*

Megan Stampfli *Embrace Diversity* pp. 735–41

1. Which of these visual arguments do you find most appealing? Least appealing? Why?

   Answers will vary.

2. Analyze the relationship between text (the words used) and the visual images and layout in each of the posters. What's the interaction between the text, on the one hand, and the visual images and layout, on the other, in each one?

   "Peeling Off Labels" uses text that looks like the label on a food package to indicate the identity contents of a person, and the image shows the label being peeled off, as though the list of identity contents is too limiting to describe a person fully.

   "Through Our Identities We Create a Community of Diversity" uses small text to make up the larger text of the word "diversity," and the silhouette images in the lower half of the poster imply a diversity of human types and experiences.

"Speak Out about Diversity" uses text to create a sense of spoken words; the lines of text radiating from the lower left-hand corner give the impression of representing speech, and the figure who seems to be jumping up mimics the explosiveness of speaking out.

"Everyone a Part, No One Apart" uses a collage of words to indicate ideas of diversity in the center of the image and frames that image with other words to lend the image a sense of order so that every word seems to be a part of one cohesive whole.

"Embracing Diversity in University Residences" uses the images of hands joined together to reflect the meaning of the words in the poem.

"Identities Are Infinite . . .What's Yours?" uses words to display multiple possibilities for identity; the image of the figure dancing in the center makes the text seem full of possibility and excitement rather than threatening.

"Embrace Diversity" uses words in collage form mixed over a picture to finish the sentence "Diversity is . . ." The words seem to make up parts of the image of the face in places.

Which poster is most effective in this regard? Why?

Answers will vary.

3. If you take each of these posters to be a definitional argument, defining diversity in some way, what argument is each making? In other words, how does each poster define *diversity?* (For a discussion of definitional arguments, see Chapter 9.)

   The posters define *diversity* as the many parts of one whole, the many aspects of identity that we all have, tapestry, the absence of bias, the acceptance of others, and seeing beyond stereotypes.

4. In defining and commenting on the notion of diversity, these posters range from approaching the topic in a didactic fashion (that is, seeking to teach a moral lesson) to approaching it much more vaguely. (Note the evaluative—and potentially negative—connotations the labels "didactic" and "vague" carry.) Choose the posters that you find most explicitly didactic and those that you

find most vague in their approach to the topic. Justify your choices. Which approach do you prefer? Why? Which do you believe is more effective in situations like this one? Why?

Answers will vary.

5–6. Writing assignments

Classroom Exercise: focus on rhetoric

Having evaluated the different posters by answering the questions at the end of the chapter, students should be aware of what they thought was effective and what wasn't. Have students create a "call for posters" that announces a poster contest at their own school. They should include a list of requirements or tips for a quality poster that will draw student attention. Students should share their requirements with the class and discuss their own experiences with school-sponsored public service ads (they might be memorable ones, inappropriate ones, ridiculous ones, and so on).

Michael Krasny and Guests *The Berkeley Bake Sale* pp. 743–54

1. How would you characterize the issues raised by California Senate Bill 185 for the College Republicans and for the Associated Students of the University of California?

   The College Republicans claim that the Senate Bill attempts to overturn the will of the voters by legislative action and institutionalizes racism, while the Associated Students claim that the Senate bill enhances diversity by allowing the admissions process to take factors such as race and gender into consideration.

   What arguments does each side offer in favor of the stance it has taken?

   The College Republicans suggest that the bill allows colleges to make race an identity marker that trumps other factors (for example, socioeconomic need) while the Associated Students suggest that SB 185 will increase diversity and address ongoing injustices in society.

   Which arguments do you find most convincing? (Note: This isn't a question about which side you most agree with. In fact, work hard to separate your own value commitments from your evaluation of the argument each side offers.) Why?

Answers will vary.

2. Not surprisingly, Krasny, a former professor of English, understood the Berkeley College Republicans' Bake Sale as a case of satire. What specifically is being satirized? How?

The College Republicans are satirizing affirmative action by offering them cheaper access to baked goods just as, they claim, minorities have easier access to college admissions because of their identity.

In fact, Krasny was careful to note that "the group has said its intent is satire," but he continues by acknowledging that "it has created a good deal of anger and even some threats." How effective do you find this act of "political theater," as Andy Nevis termed it? Why?

Answers will vary.

3. How well does Krasny moderate the interview? Do you perceive that he is balanced in his approach to the topic? That he is fair to those he is interviewing or receiving comments from? Why or why not?

Answers will vary.

In what sense is he modeling a rhetorical analysis, as discussed in Chapter 6?

Krasny presses his guests to articulate their claims and evidence as clearly as possible; see paragraph 10 for an example where Krasny asks a question that challenges an assumption behind a claim to seek further explanation.

4. Live interview programs, especially those involving more than one interviewee and more particularly those that include comments from callers or online comments, are improvisational in nature. Even the host, who is ostensibly in charge, cannot be sure where the program will end or how it will get there. The host must also monitor the passing of time. How do the constraints of this rhetorical context influence the messages or arguments that can be offered? (Chapter 1 considers rhetorical situations.)

Many answers are possible, but we note that both Andrew Nevis and Vishalli Loomba frequently repeat themselves, use filler words such as "y'know," and fail to complete some of their thoughts. Further, Vishalli Loomba's last comment, in paragraph 57, is cut off because time ran out. Had Loomba been more conscious of the time, she might have been able to offer a more focused, effective argument. In short, the constraints of radio make it difficult to offer effective arguments, especially for those who do not have a great deal of experience being on the radio.

Based on studying this transcript and perhaps your own experience, what kinds of responses to questions from interviewees or comments by listeners are most effective? Which are least effective? What can you learn about shaping effective arguments from considering these questions?

Answers will vary.

5. Writing assignment

Classroom Exercise: focus on rhetoric

Pay careful attention to how the interviewees talk on the show—the language here is far more informal than most arguments we read, especially in academic contexts. How do you react to this informality? If you find that it makes the arguments of the participants weaker, can you think of a situation where more informality is better? Try rewriting part of an argument that you've written for any class and see how the change in formality affects the argument. How does style affect substance?

Daily Californian Live Blog: "Increase Diversity Bake Sale"
pp. 756–63

1. In what ways can we think of live blogs as arguments?

A live blog is an argument because it makes a claim on our attention.

Would you categorize this live blog as an argument of fact? Of definition? Of evaluation? A causal argument? A proposal? (Chapters 8–12 discuss these categories of arguments.)

This live blog is primarily an argument of fact.

What would need to change for this live blog to become a category of argument other than the one it is?

If the live blog took sides with some of the participants or framed their reporting so that we had a better idea of the authors' position, this live blog could be a different category of argument. In other words, if this live blog offered more interpretation, it would fit into a different category of argument.

2. What are the advantages and disadvantages of live blogs as records of complex historical events like the bake sale and responses to it? In what ways are live blogs necessarily incomplete?

   A live blog is a step-by-step timeline of events, so the reader experiences the historical event in a way that more closely mirrors the actual experience of witnessing the event unfold; however, the nature of a live blog is more summary than analysis, and the brevity of its entries means that the event's complexity may be sacrificed in favor of quick-fire updates.

   How is reading a live blog as an event unfolds different from reading the blog after the event is completed?

   A blog entry written after an event takes place may offer a more framed view of what took place because the author knows how the story ends and which details are important for understanding the story's development and outcomes; live blogs cannot predict what details have the most impact on the grand scheme of the event, and instead must simply choose specifics that seem relevant at that particular moment.

3. How do the photos included as part of the blog contribute to its effectiveness? To the argument(s) it makes?

   Seeing the sheer number of protesters helps the reader visualize the strong opposition to the bake sale. The photos also help us see the racial diversity of people involved in the bake sale and subsequent protests; it is only through the photos that we learn Ward Connerly, one of the driving forces behind the bake sale, is African American, which

may surprise readers and alter their perception of the event.

4. While there was no violence at the Berkeley event, the sorts of arguments that were taking place were by no means examples of Rogerian argument as discussed in Chapter 7. Is it possible to engage in Rogerian argumentation about topics as heated as those at stake in the debates at Berkeley? Must both sides agree to use Rogerian argumentation? Why or why not?

Answers may vary, but we believe that a Rogerian argument would certainly be possible about this topic. It's not the topic itself that makes Rogerian argument difficult; it's the unwillingness of the parties involved in the debate to agree to Rogerian argument. It is possible for one side to adopt Rogerian argument without the cooperation of the other side; a speaker or writer would need to approach the argument from the perspective of having both sides win from the argument. However, if only one side adopts a Rogerian approach, it is unlikely there will be a strong sense of progress.

What might a Rogerian argument look like in this case if you contend that form of argumentation is possible here?

Such an argument would probably need to begin with some agreement about shared American values such as equality or, because both sides make frequent appeals about the importance of freedom of speech, the First Amendment.

5–6. Writing assignments

Classroom Exercise: focus on rhetoric

Academic contexts—perhaps including this textbook—often suggest that Rogerian argument is especially desirable and that more combative forms of argument are evidence of some kind of intellectual failure. In what contexts do you prefer an approach that is decidedly non-Rogerian? For example, take a look at the next article by Heather Mac Donald and think about her willful dismissal of some who disagree with her. You may not like her approach in that particular piece, but can you think of examples where being dismissive or even rude toward those who disagree might be not just entertaining but appropriate? Ask students to locate examples of writing that manages to be cutting and effective.

Heather Mac Donald *Half Baked: UC Berkeley's Diversity Machine Loses Its Mind over Cupcakes* pp. 765–66

1. Did you get new information from this selection about the bake sale at Berkeley that had not been included in the previous selections on that topic? What information is new? How does it help you understand the bake sale and the ensuing protests?

   Answers will vary.

2. Mac Donald's argument is obviously evaluative in nature. What specifically is she evaluating? (She has at least several targets.)

   Answers may vary, but they could include the following: Mac Donald evaluates Berkeley's response to the bake sale, Berkeley's vice chancellor for equity and diversity and his office, the University's position on free speech, and the academic quality of Berkeley.

   What evaluative criteria is she using?

   One of Mac Donald's criteria is reasonableness: she attacks both the students and Gibor Basri, the vice chancellor for equity and diversity, for being unreasonably offended by the bake sale and for indulging in an overheated response. One of her criteria for evaluating the University is the commitment to academic mission, a commitment that Mac Donald thinks is undermined by the University's support of an expensive diversity office.

   Which are explicitly stated and which are implicitly stated or assumed? (Chapter 10 presents information about evaluative arguments.)

   Mac Donald's criterion of reasonableness is the most clearly stated; we would suggest that the others are largely implicit.

3. How does Mac Donald use the behavior of the gender and women's studies major at the bake sale to support her claims (paragraph 4)? What specific claims is she making with this example?

   According to Mac Donald, the gender and women's studies major here reflects the desirability of being a victim on today's college campus. By pointing out this protestor,

Mac Donald claims that the outrage over the bake sale is probably fake; instead of being actually hurt or offended, many of those complaining are enjoying their moral righteousness and their opportunity to complain.

4. Describe Mac Donald's invoked audience. Is it likely that she will persuade anyone who does not already agree with her position to change theirs? Why or why not?

Answers may vary, but we would suggest that she invokes an audience of people who already agree with her and that her article does *not* have a goal of changing the minds of those who disagree with Mac Donald. For one thing, Mac Donald tends to repeat many of the standard arguments against affirmative action and life on campus and uses stereotypes of liberal and academic reactions to the bake sale.

Note at least half a dozen particular word choices that will surely appeal to those who already agree with her but that will likely alienate those who do not.

We offer a half dozen possibilities: "a storm of ludicrously clueless outrage" (paragraph 3); "the ironclad script for all such minor perturbations in the otherwise unbroken reign of campus political correctness" (paragraph 4); "the massive campus-diversity bureaucracy treat the delusional claims of hyperventilating students" (paragraph 4); "a nauseating rhetoric" (paragraph 5); "stupendously misguided interpretation" (paragraph 5); "ever-expanding diversity sinecures" (paragraph 6).

How do such word choices function as arguments based on emotion?

Our first example, "a storm of ludicrously clueless outrage" (paragraph 3) mocks the reaction that some had to the bake sale. By making the reactions seem absurd, she asks her audience to view those who reacted to the bake sale as foolish.

As arguments based on character? (Chapter 6 discusses audience, while Chapters 2 and 4 discuss arguments based on pathos and logos, respectively.)

Examples such as "campus diversity bureaucracy" and "ever-expanding diversity sinecures" signal MacDonald's no-nonsense, call-it-as-she-sees-it approach, especially to academic life. She builds an ethos of being straightforward for audiences that do not appreciate an academic's defense of nuance or contingency.

5. Writing assignment

Classroom Exercise: focus on the world

Investigate what resources your own college or university commits to diversity. Do you have a diversity officer? What kind of work does this person do? Whether your school has one or not, make an argument about the value of such a position. Does it improve the life of the institution or does it divert resources that would be better used somewhere else? By what criteria do you evaluate an office of diversity?

Tina Korbe *Remember the Racist Cupcakes? Fordham University Fights Back with Its Own Bake Sale* pp. 768–69

1. What arguments is the Fordham bake sale making?

The Fordham bake sale argues that some groups have advantages in college admissions but that these advantages are not as tied to ethnic diversity as some groups believe; instead, athletes and, especially, the wealthy are the groups who receive hidden benefits from admission offices.

In what ways is it a critique and parody of the bake sale at Berkeley?

The Fordham bake sale suggests that the Berkeley bake sale overlooks the true factors that keep college admissions from focusing on academic merit.

What motivated the Fordham bake sale?

The Fordham bake sale seems to be motivated by a desire to correct assumptions about what sort of student truly receives preferential treatment in college admissions.

2. If we analyze the Fordham bake sale as a Toulmin argument, what form would it take? (Chapter 7 discusses the structure of Toulmin arguments.)

One possibility:

Claim: College admissions actually favor the rich and the athletic more than other groups.

Reason: Statistical analysis shows that these groups receive most of the benefits.

Warrant: Statistical analysis is the best indicator of what groups actually receive benefits.

Warrant: Traditional thinking about who gets the advantages in college admissions has been wrong because it overestimates the advantages given to ethnic minorities.

Grounds: Americans believe everyone should be treated fairly.

Grounds: Statistical analysis gives us a more honest picture of what's happening in college admissions than received or assumed knowledge does.

3. How does the Fordham bake sale complicate your efforts to understand diversity on college and university campuses, especially as it relates to matters of admissions?

Answers will vary, but the Fordham bake sale probably reframes college admissions for many students who thought that race was more important than income in admission decisions.

What might it teach us about satire and controversial issues?

Answers will vary, but one lesson might be about satire's reductiveness, its tendency to focus on one element of an issue and ignore nuance. Another lesson might be that we often fall into the habit of thinking that we know what's at stake in controversial issues and so might ignore important ways of thinking about those issues; we should therefore be open to understanding issues in new ways.

139

4. Korbe is known as a political conservative, and she posted this blog entry on a Web site that identifies itself as conservative. What particular aspects of the blog posting, if any, reflect conservative thinking? How?

We would suggest that a few moments suggest conservative thinking: in the first paragraph, Korbe suggests some doubt about affirmative action and seems to challenge those who call the bake sale "racism." Also, the blog entry signals agreement with Charles Murray, a scholar usually aligned with conservative thinking. In the last paragraph, the appeal to "bring back *true* universities, centers to cultivate research and thought" signals a culturally conservative belief that the schools used to be better.

5. Writing assignment

Classroom Exercise: focus on the argument

To what degree does your institution represent one of Korbe's "true universities [or colleges]"—what she calls "centers to cultivate research and thought"? How much of your institution's success at being a place that cultivates research and thought stems from who is admitted (as opposed to how they are trained)? If your school does not, in your opinion, measure up, is that because of the way that they admit students? What would a better admission system look like? Is it OK for admissions to be biased or should they strive for some sort of objectivity?

Jennifer Delahunty Britz *To All the Girls I've Rejected* pp. 771–72

1. What were your responses to this selection? Were you aware of the issues it deals with? What were your intellectual responses, that is, those based on reason or knowledge? What were your affective responses, that is, those based on feelings or attitudes?

Answers will vary.

2. What arguments is Britz making in this essay?

Britz argues that well-qualified young women are being denied admission to selective colleges because of the increasing competitiveness among young women.

Are her arguments focused primarily on the past, the future, or the present? Why?

Her arguments are largely focused on the present because she is describing the current college admission situation, including her own daughter's experiences. However, many of her arguments are about the future because she is asking questions about what might happen in the years to come as the gender imbalance gets worse. Finally, she is also arguing about the past and how the current situation is different from the situation of a couple of decades ago.

Who are Britz's audiences? Consider here not only her title but also how she frames her comments. To whom does she seem to be writing? (See Chapter 1 for a discussion of occasions for argument and Chapter 6 for a discussion of audience.)

We would suggest that she's writing more to parents and to adults who are out of college than she is to those who have received rejection letters; she is not explaining how to get into college, after all, but what the process looks like and how the demographics are changing.

3. How does Britz use personal experience in this essay to create arguments based on emotion, character, and facts and logic? A useful way to think about this question will be to consider the different roles that Britz has now and in the past with respect to the issues she is discussing. (Chapters 2–4 discuss arguments based on pathos, ethos, and logos, respectively.)

In terms of pathos, Britz offers the experience of dealing with her daughter's disappointment as a way of building an emotional bridge with her audience. In terms of ethos, Britz appeals to her experience as the mother of a daughter who received a rejection letter and so has firsthand experience of the disappointment *and* as a hard-working director of admissions who has to make difficult decisions. In terms of logos, Britz relies on the sort of statistics that a college admissions officer would know (see, for example, paragraph 8) as well as making the logical argument in paragraphs 10–12 about the importance of gender balance; these are arguments that depend on her experience as a college admissions officer.

4. Explain the humor in the visual illustration that appeared with this column when it was first published. How does the visual play on words contribute to its humor?

The play on words focuses on the "I can't" that appears in the word "applicant" (with the comma after "applicant" turning into an apostrophe), and it reinforces the idea in the article that the admissions officers would like to be able to make offers to many accomplished young women but demographics keep them from being able to accept many of the qualified women who apply (that is, it reinforces an idea of "I can't admit you" because of demographic trends rather than the idea that the students who were rejected did something wrong or were weak candidates).

How is it relevant to the argument the article is making?

We would suggest that the graphic is relevant given the explanation that the graphic emphasizes that the admission officers would prefer to be able to offer admission but feel like they can't in many cases.

5. Writing assignment

Classroom Exercise: focus on the argument

Looking around the campus, do students notice a difference in the number of males compared to the number of females? Have men in the class felt like a minority at any point? Have women noticed a general lack of men on campus? Is there a public policy about male recruitment on campus? What do students think will draw men to campus, and what lengths do they think are appropriate for their school? Is it important to maintain a minimum number of men at the university? Why? This debate parallels that over affirmative action for minority students, but how might these situations be different?

Scott Jaschik *Affirmative Action for Men*   pp. 774–79

1. What arguments is Jaschik making in this article?

Jaschik argues that the issue of gender balance on campus —and therefore the related issues of possible affirmative action for men—is incredibly complicated, both legally and ethically.

How does he begin with Britz's column, the previous selection, "To All the Girls I've Rejected," using it as a springboard for discussing a range of related issues?

Britz's column provides Jaschik with an explanation for why his argument is timely; her article provides the context for why he would argue about these issues.

What do we learn from Jaschik's article about the complex nature of the issues involved as various groups and individuals understand them?

Answers will vary, but many students will learn that the issue goes far beyond choosing who gets into the college to include issues of how we think about the purpose of education and how we handle admissions and other aspects of higher education both legally and ethically.

2. Jaschik discusses his topic from two perspectives, a legal one and an ethical one. What relationship, if any, is there between these two perspectives?

The most important relationship is probably the distinction between the two: the difference between what is legal (what *can* colleges do) and what is ethical (what *should* they do). In most cases, schools will need to decide how to fit the two issues together, to figure out what they should do and how much of what they feel they should do is permissible by law.

Why is this an interesting way to treat the topic, given the likely audience of *Inside Higher Ed*?

Most of Jaschik's audience will likely be those who work in higher education—that is, the people reading the article are likely to wonder about what their own institution both can and should do.

3. Comments in paragraph 4 and 5 of this article make clear that some groups were surprised that Britz had spoken publicly about the issue of admissions and the gender gap on campus. Which groups were surprised?

Jaschik mentions that applicants and parents were surprised by the content of the article, and those who work in college admissions and those who work with education law

were surprised that Britz wrote about the topic in a main-stream media outlet.

How does their surprise offer readers insight into the issue itself?

Their surprise makes it clear that many people who work in higher education do not think that this is a topic that should be talked about publicly.

Why might one group have wanted to talk on background about the topic?

Lawyers in particular understand that speaking about issues that are subject to litigation can make one the subject of litigation; that is, lawyers do not want to get involved and take a position before they have had time to do research and sort out their own arguments.

4. As is often the case in online contexts, Jaschik's articles received many comments. Here is an interesting one by someone who identifies himself as "Joe Counselor":

> I am an admission counselor at a "highly selective" small, residential, liberal arts college, similar to Kenyon. In reading the postings, I felt the need to chime in with a few points.
>
> . . ."Name withheld upon request" offered a great point in an earlier post. S/he said, "The vast majority (I'd say upwards of 85%) of the applicants we received were 'qualified' to do the work at the college." This is the case at my institution, as I'm sure it is at a lot of other institutions. Most of our applicants are extremely bright, receive great grades, and test very well. We received 3,588 applications for a total of 265 spots, so how are we to differentiate between applicants? You advocated using a system where SATs and grades are the only factors. As idealistic and nice as that is, you completely overlook differences between high schools. I speak not just of the differences between the "haves" and the "have-nots" but also, for example, certain elite private high schools are notorious for grade deflation. You cited AP and IB credits. . . .what about high schools that do not offer AP or IB designated classes? I realize one could prepare on their own for the exam, but by now, hopefully my point comes across clearly—there is no objective "be all, end all" solution available.
>
> A second issue that was not discussed is institutional priorities. Colleges are businesses. Students and their parents are

paying customers. I often get asked the question, "What is the difference between your college and X college?" Parents want to know why they should pay 30k–40k a year to send Junior to my institution. Differentiation is a simple reality and colleges seek a diverse crop of students not just for the potential to improve their campus life and discussion, etc., but for other bonuses. A 50/50 male female balance is good for campus dynamics AND parents like hearing that during information sessions. They like hearing 70/30 in-state/out-of-state ratio, or that 36% of our students are students of color because Junior will be exposed to students with different backgrounds. Like most colleges and universities, our President and Board of Trustees have given us a few things to think about while reading. Obviously, our chief goal is to admit a great academic class, but we're also charged with shaping a class that offers more than just 265 academic all-stars. We need quarterbacks, dancers, pianists, etc. . . . And then development office likes to weigh in from time to time with "special cases". . . after all, who doesn't want a new science building or athletic facility on campus?

In short, let's not go crucifying Ms. Britz for what she wrote. At a school that looks to fill 441 spots from a pool of 3,929, all the while appeasing the president, the development office, the alums, the coaches, and (apparently) the masses, she does a pretty great job.

How do Joe Counselor's remarks complicate an already complicated situation? In other words, what new relevant information does he add to our understanding of the set of issues being addressed?

These remarks underscore many factors about admission that go unmentioned in the article such as the difficulty of developing an objective system for ranking and identifying candidates, the diversity of skills desired on campus, the desire of parents to hear particular statistics about colleges, and the conflicting interests (presidents, development offices, etc.) that can influence admissions decisions.

What sorts of arguments does Joe Counselor offer? Are his arguments based on emotion, character, or facts and reasons?

Joe Counselor's arguments are, to a significant degree, based on character: he reports that he works in college admissions, and his explanation of the inner workings of

admissions suggests that he is knowledgeable. Moreover, his generosity toward others in praising both "Name withheld upon request" and Jennifer Delahunty Britz build his ethos as a thoughtful writer. The more powerful arguments, perhaps, are those based on facts and reasons; Joe Counselor explains the complicated world of college admissions in clear, comprehensible terms.

How do they compare with the sorts of arguments often made in comments posted online in response to articles?

Among the possible answers: these arguments seem much more fully developed than most online responses, and the comments are surprisingly positive about the other commenter that Joe Counselor refers to as well as the author of the original article.

5. Writing assignment

Classroom Exercise: focus on the world

Does gender representation matter in education? Thinking about your own experience in education, construct an argument about how gender does or does not matter in thinking about the composition of an educational community. Does it matter how old the students are? Is gender balance, or even single-sex education, more appropriate for some age and grade levels than it is for others?

Libby Sander *Blue-Collar Boomers Take Work Ethic to College* pp. 782–85

1. What argument(s) is Libby Sander making in this selection?

Sander argues that an increasing number of blue-collar workers are returning to school, usually to get better jobs.

What factors account for the situation that she is describing?

She focuses on returning students who are seeking work that is less physically demanding or pays more.

To what extent are these older Americans becoming students as a matter of choice? As a matter of necessity?

It's sometimes unclear precisely what role choice and necessity play in these decisions; necessity sounds tremendously

important for some of the returning students, though many have clearly made a choice.

As Sander describes the situation, in what ways does social class intersect with the values that these students bring to school with them?

Her article suggests that these students who have labored at physically demanding jobs for years bring a work ethic and a no-nonsense approach that will help them in school.

2. As noted, this article was written before the economic downturn of 2008. How has the economic situation in the United States changed since that time?

   Answers to this question will vary depending on when students read this article.

   Do you believe that these changes have had any influence on who is attending college or why? What evidence might you offer for your position?

   Answers will vary.

3. What sorts of evidence does Sander present to support her claims?

   Sander relies on some surveys but mostly on personal interviews.

   How might her article have been different if she had relied only on, let's say, statistics?

   The story would have had a much less personal tone and made fewer emotional appeals.

   How would the tone of the article, for example, have been different?

   Her tone might have been more academic and, arguably, drier and less interesting.

4. How does the presence of older Americans on campus change the nature of college life? How might the life experiences of people like Russell Kearney, David Cox, and Dannie Hill influence their behavior as students? How might they influence the nature or content of class discussions, for example? What advantages

might there be to having a student population that is not all of a single age cohort?

Answers will vary, but we would suggest that older students often bring more seriousness and sense of purpose to their studies; Sander's argument certainly supports that view. One advantage of a more diverse cohort of students in terms of age is that older students might bring an ability to make concrete connections between what students learn in school and how they live the rest of their lives. On the other hand, younger students might bring an enthusiasm and an ability to question that will complement the learning patterns of the older students.

5. Writing assignment

Classroom Exercise: focus on the world

Interview a few people who are older than you about their experience with higher education. If your interviewee did not go to college, does he or she regret it? What led to the choice not to attend? (Did it even feel like a choice at the time?) If your interviewee did attend, what advice would he or she give to students attending now? Share the advice that you collected with that advice collected by your other classmates. Do patterns emerge? Could you use the advice that older people gave you about college?

Edward F. Palm *The Veterans Are Coming! The Veterans Are Coming!* pp. 788–94

1. In what ways is Palm's essay a proposal argument?

Palm first identifies a potential problem (that campuses will not know how to handle an influx of veterans on campus) and offers specific solutions for how to solve the problem (the five pieces of advice with which he ends the article).

What does he propose?

He proposes five guidelines for making a campus welcoming for veterans: treat veterans like any other students; don't thank veterans for their service if you don't know them; don't shy away from political discussions in class; don't ask about their war experience but wait for them to

decide if they want to speak about it; and expect veterans to succeed.

What situation leads him to offer his proposal?

The most immediate situation is the passage of a new GI Bill that will support the desire of many veterans to get a college education. Palm's own experience as a veteran and an academic has also influenced him to make this proposal.

How appropriate do you find Palm's advice? (For a discussion of proposal argument, see Chapter 12.)

Answers will vary.

2. The first half of Palm's essay is based on personal experiences. In what ways does Palm use these experiences to construct logical arguments? Ethical arguments? Emotional arguments? (For a discussion of these kinds of arguments, see Chapters 4, 3, and 2, respectively.) An interesting way to think about this question would be to consider what the essay would be like if it began with paragraph 15.

One example of a logical argument would be Palm's argument that students who have experienced boot camp would better appreciate the opportunity to get an education. Palm builds on his own experience as a veteran to get us to trust his knowledge of what it means to be a veteran who attends college. In writing about his youthful experiences as a Marine, and of another young man who went back home after a few weeks of boot camp, he also builds an emotional bridge by reminding readers of their own youth and how difficult it could be to make sense of life then.

3. One resource that writers of arguments have is their readers' knowledge of earlier texts, events, and situations. By referring to specific things that readers know, writers communicate more than they explicitly say. (*Intertextuality* is the technical label for this relationship, especially when it involves relationships between written texts or text-like things, such as films.) Palm takes advantage of this fact throughout this essay. How, for example, does an understanding of the allusion in the title, the poem by Kipling, the New Testament story of Paul, the *Rambo* novel and the movies it inspired, and the Roth short story strengthen and

enrich Palm's argument? How does such intertextuality contribute to Palm's ethos?

Answers will vary, but we would offer a couple of suggestions about how the stories affect his argument and his ethos. First, we would suggest that when he mentions the _Rambo_ novel and movies, Palm comes across as knowledgeable about one way that popular culture imagines veterans, as driven nearly crazy by their desire for revenge. When he quotes the Kipling poem, Palm perhaps comes across as well educated, as it's not a particularly famous poem (the same might be true of the Roth story). The poem also establishes a tradition of asking people to think about veterans first and foremost as people. The mention of the road to Damascus might allow Palm to connect with more religious readers, and it establishes an understanding that joining military culture could be such an affecting event that it is like a spiritual conversion.

What is missed by readers who do not have knowledge of these texts, events, or situations?

Answers will vary, but they might miss out on some of the dimensions of meaning suggested in the answers to the previous questions.

4. Giving advice to others, especially people you do not know well, is always a challenging rhetorical task. How well does Palm do? Consider the tone that he uses in the final third of the essay, where he gives "five pieces of common sense advice" (paragraph 20). How would you characterize it? Do you find the tone effective? Why or why not?

Answers will vary, but we find the tone to be fair-minded and polite while still authoritative. One piece of evidence that he is fair-minded is that he mentions that both members of the military and college administrators can be overbearing or excessively kind; that is, they do not conform to easy stereotypes. One piece of evidence that he is authoritative would be that his recommendations are directive without entertaining lots of alternative possibilities.

5–6. Writing assignments

Classroom Exercise: focus on the world

If you're not a veteran, what do you think about Palm's concern that campuses might not be veteran-friendly? Based on your experience, is there reason to have doubts about how professors and administrators might treat veterans? What about other students? If you are a veteran, what has your experience on campus been like? Do you agree with Palm's suggestions? Do you have suggestions for making your campus more welcoming to veterans?

Patricia Cohen *Professors' Liberalism Contagious? Maybe*
Not pp. 796–98

1. The first half of this article contends that an "article of faith" among certain critics of American higher education may, in fact, be false. What is the article of faith, and what arguments and evidence does Cohen cite that may undercut it?

   The article of faith is "that liberal professors politically indoctrinate their students" (paragraph 1). Cohen cites research from Fritschler, Mayer, and Smith; Woessner and Kelly-Woessner; and Mariani and Hewitt. All of these researchers say that there is no evidence of indoctrination.

2. The second half of this article takes a different turn, arguing that there is, indeed, a problem on American campuses but a problem of a very different nature. According to this section of the article, what is the real problem?

   The second half of the article suggests that the problem is "academic groupthink" on campus and that there is not enough diversity of political opinion on the faculty or enough teaching of traditional subjects.

   Cohen closes this article by indirectly quoting A. Lee Fritschler: "If anything . . . the problem is not too much politics, but too little" (paragraph 19). What does Fritschler mean by this statement?

   Fritschler means that there is not enough engagement in civic and political affairs.

   What would you imagine Fritschler's own political values and commitments to be? Why?

Answers may vary—be sure to press students to provide evidence for their opinions (they might, for example, look up the associations of his publisher).

3. In paragraph 15, Cohen quotes K. C. Johnson: "The conservative critics are inventing a straw man that doesn't exist and are missing the real problem that does." What does Johnson mean?

Johnson thinks that the concern over political indoctrination is the wrong concern to have because the real problem is the loss of traditional areas of intellectual inquiry.

What is a straw man when one is discussing arguments?

A straw man is an argument, weaker or more extreme than the real argument one wants to dismiss, that is created because it is easier to knock down than the real argument.

Does it involve ethical, emotional, or logical appeals? Why?

A straw man is usually considered a fallacy of logical argument because it fails to treat the logic of the real argument honestly.

What is the specific straw man that Johnson contends is being created in this situation? (For a discussion of fallacies of argument, including a straw man argument, see Chapter 5.)

Johnson thinks that the idea that professors are indoctrinating students is the straw man because that's not the threat that he thinks really matters.

4. Cohen mentions the American Council of Trustees and Alumni (paragraph 16) and the National Association of Scholars (paragraph 18). Do some research on these two organizations to discover their positions and the values to which they are committed. In light of this research, evaluate Anne Neal's claim that "it is not about left and right." In other words, based on your research, would you expect that most of the members of these two organizations are politically conservative and therefore affiliated with the right or politically liberal and therefore affiliated with the left? Why?

Answers may vary depending on how students interpret the evidence, but both organizations are generally recognized as politically conservative and associated with the right.

Is this information relevant to Neal's claim? Why or why not?

Answers may vary, though we tend to think it's relevant, especially if we consider professors' political views to be relevant.

5. Writing assignment

Classroom Exercise: focus on rhetoric

Cohen is careful to interview subjects who disagree in some way with the primary claim that professors indoctrinate students. Evaluate her choice of whom to interview. Is she choosing sources that you trust to have an informed opinion? Now take a look at a news source that you generally trust and evaluate how a few different stories balance the claims of opposing opinions. Do all stories need to be told from two sides? Does this tactic present any weaknesses or problems? Do you feel that the media source that you examined is generally fair in the presentation of news, or do you think that you trust them because they usually confirm things you want to hear?

Mack D. Mariani and Gordon J. Hewitt
Indoctrination U.? Faculty Ideology and Changes in Student Political Orientation (Excerpt) pp. 801–7

1. One purpose of this research was to use the statistical analysis of data gathered from students to test a claim that is commonly made by conservative critics of American universities. What claim is being tested? State this claim as a Toulmin argument. (For a discussion of Toulmin argumentation, see Chapter 7.)

Answers may vary. We offer the following.

Claim: We should change higher education in the United States in some way (for example, Horowitz wants to add the Academic Bill of Rights while others want to hire more professors who are conservative).

Reason: Students at American colleges and universities are being indoctrinated by left-wing professors.

Warrant: Students should not be subject to political indoctrination.

Backing: Students should be allowed to think for themselves in college. Classrooms are appropriate for studying

153

academic subjects, not for listening to professors spout off their political opinions.

2. What did Mariani and Hewitt find when they tested the claim discussed in question 1?

   They found there was little evidence that students' political views were changing over their college careers.

   What is the difference between a purely logical argument (as discussed in question 1) and one that is based on empirical data (as is the case in this research)?

   Most of all, the arguments depend on different kinds of evidence. For example, those who claim that professors indoctrinate students might be right that professors are left-wingers and that students are in vulnerable positions, but that still doesn't mean that the students will be converted by the professors. (Students might be savvy about negotiating the attempted conversion, or professors might be bad at indoctrinating.) The logical theory about how professors might be changing students doesn't provide the same information as the empirical evidence that measures actual changes.

3. Briefly outline the "Discussion" section of this selection to get a clear idea how it is structured. In outlining, you are looking for the major topic of each paragraph and the way that the paragraphs work together to conclude the article. Based on this particular "Discussion" section, how would you characterize the functions of a discussion section of a research article? In other words, how is this section structured and why?

   The "Discussion" section first summarizes the findings of the research, then considers how those data are or are not surprising, then discusses the limitations of the research, and then summarizes the most important findings. The structure lets us see what the research teaches us, acknowledges that it is not perfect, and ends with a reconsideration of what the research means and how we should think about the information.

4. A particularly interesting aspect of this article and one that empirical researchers very much appreciate is the way that it qualifies claims, as discussed in Chapter 7. Analyze paragraph 8 in this regard by first copying the paragraph and then underlining any language that can be seen as a qualification of a claim. Compare your results with those of a classmate. Likewise, discuss why the qualified claims made here are ultimately stronger and less subject to criticism than are unqualified claims.

Answers may vary, especially in discussion of the qualifications to the argument. See example below.

Though we are hopeful that this study contributes to ongoing debates about faculty ideology and indoctrination, there are some limitations to this study that should be taken into account by other researchers. We are mindful, for instance, that our finding that students move leftward during college is not, by itself, evidence of indoctrination. Students may move to the left as a result of other factors, such as shared cultural influences, a common stage in personal development, or as a reaction to peer pressure, current events, or political developments. We have tried to deal with this problem by controlling for faculty ideology; if faculty ideology has an impact on student ideology then changes in student ideology should be more pronounced at institutions with more liberal faculty members and vice versa. We find little evidence that this is the case. Of course, this finding does not necessarily mean that professors act fairly or without ideological bias in their teachings, subject matter, or selection of reading materials. Professors could, after all, but *failing* to indoctrinate students despite their concerted efforts to do so! Regardless of any biases (intentional or unintentional) that professors bring to their teaching, the findings presented here may help alleviate the concern that students, on a widespread basis, are adopting the political positions of their liberal professors.

5. A large part of the "Discussion" section describes the limitations of the research. How does this discussion contribute to the researchers' ethos? In what ways does an acknowledgment of the limitations of a research study function like qualifiers in an argument?

The discussion of limitations enhances the authors' ethos by showing that they understand that there might be limitations to what their research can establish. The acknowledgment of limitations functions just like qualifiers in an argument because this acknowledgment places limits on the claims and the responsibilities of the arguments.

How does the authors' note—the unnumbered footnote indicated by an asterisk—contribute to their ethos? (For a discussion of ethos, see Chapter 3. For a discussion of qualifiers, see Chapter 7.)

This note is likely to enhance the authors' ethos greatly by suggesting that the research team does not have the goal of supporting only one side in this debate and that they have a balanced approach to the question.

6. Writing assignment

Classroom Exercise: focus on the argument

Compare this article with the previous news article that summarizes the results of several studies on faculty ideology. What features of the argument mark Mariani and Hewitt's article as academic argument? What are the strengths of academic argument on an issue like this? What are the strengths of the less academic argument presented by Cohen? Which argument do you find more compelling? Why? In what contexts and with what audiences might the argument that you find less compelling actually be more persuasive?

Walter Benn Michaels *The Trouble with Diversity: How We Learned to Love Identity and Ignore Inequality* pp. 809–14

1. What, for Walter Benn Michaels, is the real issue that American society needs to confront?

Economic inequality.

How, for him, does defining *diversity* in terms of a celebration of difference, especially ethnic difference, prevent Americans from both seeing the real issue and doing anything about it?

The celebration of difference means that we don't pay attention to the importance of eliminating differences such as income inequality.

In what ways does our society's focus on ethnic and cultural diversity necessarily perpetuate racism and biological essentialism (paragraph 10)?

This focus makes us believe in the idea of racial identity and related values, not allowing us to question whether there even are biological differences between different races.

2. Why and how are these issues relevant to discussions of diversity on campus in general?

Michaels is arguing for a different way of thinking about diversity, not for discounting the value of diversity. How a campus defines diversity determines what kind of diversity it will pursue—which students it will recruit, give scholarship money to, and so forth.

On the campus you attend?

Answers will vary.

3. Later in this introduction, Michaels, a liberal, points out ways in which both conservatives and liberals in American public life, first, focus on racial or ethnic differences rather than issues of social inequality and, second, benefit from doing so. In a 2004 essay, "Diversity's False Solace," he notes:

[W]e like policies like affirmative action not so much because they solve the problem of racism but because they tell us that racism is the problem we need to solve. . . . It's not surprising that universities of the upper middle class should want their students to feel comfortable [as affirmative action programs enable and encourage them to do]. What is surprising is that diversity should have become the hallmark of liberalism.

Analyze the argument made in this paragraph as a Toulmin argument. (For a discussion of Toulmin argumentation, see Chapter 7.)

Answers may vary, but we offer this possibility:

Claim: Diversity should not be the hallmark of liberalism.

Reason: Diversity is more about making people feel good about themselves than it is about solving a problem.

Warrant: Liberals should care about solving problems, not about making people feel good about themselves.

Backing: Liberals are devoted to the common good.

4. How would you characterize Michaels's argument? In what ways is it an argument of fact?

Michaels traces some of the history of the interest in diversity to argue for how we have come to the understanding that we have now.

A definitional argument?

Michaels argues that we define diversity in one particular way and he wants to offer a new definition for us to use.

An evaluative argument?

Michaels evaluates the current state of our pursuit of equality.

A causal argument?

Michaels examines why we think the way that we do today and what problems result from that way of thinking.

A proposal? (For a discussion of these kinds of arguments, see Chapters 8–12.)

Michaels is proposing a new way of thinking about what constitutes diversity and a new way of achieving the goal of social justice; he implies other proposal arguments about changing our institutions, too, but this introduction doesn't spell those proposals out.

5. Writing assignment

Classroom Exercise: focus on the argument

For whom is Michaels writing? Do you think that his argument will appeal to conservatives? To liberals? To libertarians? What audience do you think is his intended audience? Who is his invoked audience? What evidence can you cite for your answers to these questions? Research some of the reviews of Michaels's book that came out when the book was published or reader reviews that appear on Amazon.com or bn.com. What kind of audience is most receptive to his argument? Why?

Wrap-up Exercises for "What Should 'Diversity on Campus' Mean and Why?"

These final assignments are provided as an opportunity to reflect on the readings as a whole and to construct arguments based on what students have taken away from the selections. Question 3 is appropriate for use as an in-class essay.

1. Investigate the diversity mission at your institution by looking at various Web sites and statistics that may be published. Then look for any news items over the years that chronicle your school's history of minority inclusion. Write an essay in which you evaluate the progress or lack of progress that you see in the school's definition of diversity and its handling of diversity.

2. Interview five to ten students at your institution about their views of the liberal or conservative nature of the school. Concentrate on interviewing individuals who probably hold different political ideals than your own to familiarize yourself with that point of view with regard to your own environment. Find out how they view the institution as a whole, as well as other students, professors, and the level of ideology in the classroom, and also uncover their ideas about remedying any problems that they see. Use what you learn to write an essay in which you evaluate their claims and present what you understand to be happening on campus.

3. Write an essay about how you would increase the cultural diversity of a student body or the ideological diversity of a faculty if you were the head of a committee charged with presenting possible tools for increasing diversity without using affirmative action. Alternatively, construct an argument for affirmative action as the best way to increase either student or faculty diversity.

CHAPTER 26

What Are You Working For?

The readings in this chapter explore how work fits into our lives and how we think we should prepare students for their working lives. Some students, of course, are deeply enmeshed in the world of work right now; for others, the world of work is something separate from their student lives, something they will only encounter once they graduate. In either case, most of these readings should not feel like an abstract discussion of issues that don't pertain to students, for they address issues that will affect every student at some point.

Some of the readings here are most concerned with making a living, but most ask questions about how our work constitutes part of ourselves. Some of the questions that the chapter raises include the following:

- How does work fit into a life? What portion of our time and energy should we devote to work?
- What makes work meaningful? What kinds of work are worth doing?
- How should education relate to work? What education should young people get for their working lives? What education should we be willing to pay for to prepare young people?

Dave Isay, editor *Dr. Monica Mayer, 45, Interviewed by Her Cousin and Patient, Spencer Wilkinson Jr., 39*   pp. 818–19
Ken Kobus, 58, Tells His Friend Ron Baraff, 42, about Making Steel   pp. 819–21

1. Although we generally don't think of stories as argument, they all express points of view. (In fact, everything is an argument, if we believe the title of this book.) Summarize the arguments made by each of these narratives.

Answers will vary. One possibility for the Monica Mayer narrative is that she argues for the importance of teaching children to work hard through tough love. For Ken Kobus's narrative, the argument might be that even difficult, dangerous jobs can be beautiful and enjoyable.

2. What does each narrative teach us about work and dedication?

Answers will vary, but the first narrative might teach us that hard physical labor is undesirable and that hard work in the academic arena will offer different rewards. The second narrative describes a great deal of beauty and happiness in the physical labor involved in steelwork.

3. In her interview, does Monica Mayer sound like a doctor as she talks? Why or why not? Is her language appropriate to the context and audience? Why or why not? Would her story have been different if she had used more formal language? Would it have been as effective? Why or why not? (For a discussion of style in arguments, see Chapter 13.)

Answers will vary, but we think that Mayer doesn't sound much like a doctor because she uses colloquial and informal language ("half-breed," "bust my head twice up against the brick wall"). However, we also think that the tone is appropriate for a story about growing up told to a younger relative. Telling this story in more formal language would have reduced its immediacy and the feeling of what it was like for Mayer as a young girl.

4. One of Ken Kobus's arguments is that "steelmaking is just beautiful" (paragraph 3). Was such a claim surprising for you? Why? What evidence does Kobus offer? For him, what is the nature of the beauty of steelmaking? (It is, for example, not like the beauty of flowers in spring or a child's face.) In what ways is his discussion of this issue a definitional argument? (For a discussion of definitional argument, see Chapter 9.)

Answers will vary, but one possibility is that Kobus redefines the work of steelmaking as a kind of art; his language sounds something like the description of the materials in, for example, glassblowing or sculpting. If any students are familiar with arguments about the sublime, they might

argue that Kobus explains steelmaking according to those aesthetics—steelmaking as great and awe-inspiring.

5. Writing assignment

Classroom Exercise: focus on the world

Ask students to interview each other about their own work experiences and write down the narratives. What kinds of arguments are made by the students' stories of their working histories? What do we learn from the narratives that the students created?

Lisa W. Foderaro *The Well-to-Do Get Less So, and Teenagers Feel the Crunch* pp. 823–26

1. What challenges did the economic downturn present to the teenagers who are discussed in Lisa W. Foderaro's article?

Several of the teenagers had to cut down on their discretionary spending, some had to find work, and some were unable to find work.

In what ways were teenagers from different social classes similarly affected?

Teenagers from different social classes had their allowances cut and so sought work.

In what ways were the effects different? Were the differences purely quantitative (that is, different degrees of the same effects) or were they qualitative (that is, different kinds of effects)? How and why?

Answers will vary, but we would suggest that having one's $5-per-week allowance cut is a qualitative difference from having one's allowance cut from $100 to $60 per week. From the sound of things, the young man whose $5 allowance was cut is part of a family that is in much more serious financial difficulty than the families of the teenagers who are the focus of this article; he's expected to make contributions to the family income, not just to earn money for the things he desires.

2. The article discusses the ways that high school students are expected to create a particular kind of ethos as college applicants.

What consequences, if any, do you think the economic downturn might have on this application process and these expectations? Why?

Answers will vary; one possibility is that more students may apply with work experience instead of volunteer experience. In that case students may need to be more careful to explain how an entry-level job gave them important experiences as a way of building their ethos.

3. The graphic "Teenage Workers" did not appear in the print version of this article but was included in the online version. Are there aspects of the graphic that you find surprising?

Answers will vary.

These figures are for teens who did paid work outside the home. Work that is not paid officially (taxed by the government) is not included. Thus, work done around the house, on most farms, or in a family business was not shown on this graphic. What information does the graphic contribute to the article that is not already included in the written text?

This graphic offers historical perspectives on teen unemployment over a few decades.

The graph on the left, "Teens in the work force," is discussed in some detail in the article, but the graph on the right, "Gap in unemployment rates," is not. Write a paragraph in which you describe this graphic as you would if you were using it to construct an argument of your own.

Answers will vary.

4–5. Writing assignments

Classroom Exercise: focus on the world

Should teenagers be expected to work outside the home? Should low-wage, low-skilled work be considered a positive factor in a college application, or should students opt for volunteer positions? Do students who do not work develop an acceptable work ethic? If your students are traditional college-age students, they should have some authority for speaking about these questions in a roundtable discussion or class debate. If they're older, nontraditional students, they might even have stronger opinions about whether teenagers should work outside the home and what costs and benefits such work entails.

Rebecca Mead *Learning by Degrees [and Live Chat with the Author]*   pp. 828–38

1. Characterize Mead's argument in "Learning by Degrees." What is her central claim?

Mead claims that there are other measures for the value of an education besides income potential.

What evidence does she provide for her position?

At the end of paragraph 7 she lists several things that an education accomplishes in addition to preparing one for a job: "to nurture critical thought; to expose individuals to the signal accomplishments of humankind; to develop in them an ability not just to listen actively but to respond intelligently."

How does she deal with potential criticisms of her position or alternative positions on the issues she is discussing? In what ways does she qualify her claims?

She includes evidence that studying things that aren't engineering or accounting can still provide one with the ability to make a reasonable living (see paragraph 8, where she mentions that philosophy majors average $40,000 as a starting salary).

How does doing so strengthen her argument? (See Chapter 7 for information on structuring arguments.)

In defending the non-economic advantages of higher education she's careful to point out that the economic advantages still matter.

2. What sorts of evidence does Mead use in presenting information in "Learning by Degrees"? Make a list of all the kinds of evidence she uses as well as the sources she provides for that information.

Mead uses inartistic arguments when she draws salary statistics from Payscale.com. She cites two academic authorities, Richard Vedder and Robert Lerman, both quoted in the *New York Times*, and she cites political sources, including

Peggy Noonan, Sarah Palin, Charles Murray, and President Obama, all quoted from the popular media. Mead's artistic arguments usually involve qualifying or finding objections to the claims of others.

How do her use and presentation of evidence contribute to her ethos? (See Chapters 7 and 17 on evidence and Chapter 3 on ethos in arguments.)

Answers may vary, though we would suggest that Mead develops a confident, authoritative ethos as someone who can question the "wisdom" of academic and political experts, as someone who can marshal figures to support her claims, and as someone who can creatively use evidence and style to build her argument.

3. Try to summarize the arguments that are being made by the people posting comments in the live chat with Mead. If you read carefully, you've already noticed that some people besides Mead posted more than once. (Here, it may be easiest to begin by listing the main point of each comment or question that is posted and then to try to group those points into categories. You may end up with a visual diagram that lists the major arguments and shows the relationships among them using spatial arrangement and conventions like arrows.) Do you find this task easy or challenging? Why might this be the case?

Answers will vary.

4. How do such electronically mediated interactions permit new kinds of arguments to take place in the public arena?

Answers will vary, but among the possibilities is the idea that electronic interactions have a democratizing influence; almost anyone can write in and comment on Rebecca Mead's argument because access to the Internet is widely available. However, Mead often seems to offer responses that are quite short, as though she does not have much time for each individual.

How might we characterize such interactions? How, for example, are they like or not like face-to-face interactions?

Answers will vary, but among the possibilities is the idea that electronic interactions tend to be short and not allow

as much time for qualifying claims as face-to-face interactions might offer. Also, even though Mead is careful to call some of the writers by name and offer personal encouragement, the electronic interactions are less personal because of the lack of face-to-face interaction; Mead doesn't really get to know anyone who writes her a question.

5. Writing assignment

Classroom Exercise: focus on the world

Why are your students in college? How much do they care about educational practices that are not pre-professional? Can they make an argument for the value of the liberal arts? How would they articulate the value of classes or subjects that are not pre-professional, if at all? You might stage an in-class debate on the value of a liberal arts education and then have students write a reflection piece on why they study what they study and what they hope for from their college education.

Making a Visual Argument: Spotlight on Statistics: Back to College

U.S. Bureau of Labor Statistics *College Students and Graduates* and *The College and University Workplace* pp. 839–51

1. In what ways might we read the information provided about each of the topics treated as an argument?

   Each of these graphs makes a claim about how we should see the world; some are arguments to inform (for example, "Degree Attainment by Age 22") while others seem designed to be more persuasive (for example, ". . .and Higher Earnings," especially when considered in light of the comments above the graph, seems designed to encourage students to pursue a college education).

   Do these arguments work together to form an argument or several arguments at some more abstract level? (Consider, for example, why the topics are arranged in the order that they are. Their ordering doesn't seem to be haphazard or random. Does there

167

appear to be some sequence to the arrangement of at least some of these topics?)

The first three arguments suggest that higher education is a worthwhile investment. The arguments collected under the rubric "The College and University Workplace" seem to suggest that pursuing a career working in a higher education is a good idea because education offers growth in the number of jobs, good wages, and safe working conditions.

2. Were you surprised by the information presented about any of these topics? Which one(s) and why?

Answers will vary.

3. How could these figures be used to support arguments about the value of education and especially higher education?

These figures suggest that a college education is worth the investment of time and money because of the employment security and income that a college education provides.

Which specific figures would be most useful?

The first three graphs—about increasing employment, lower unemployment, and higher earnings—would be the most useful for supporting arguments about the value of higher education.

What claims could they be used to support?

These figures would be especially useful for supporting claims about the economic benefits of higher education (for purposes of class discussion, you might point out that these graphs don't provide any evidence for the intellectual, emotional, social, etc. benefits of higher education; that is, they present support for only one kind of evidence).

4. Examine closely the figure "Mean Annual Earnings and Employment of Selected Postsecondary Teachers in Colleges and Universities, May 2009." Although there is no reason to doubt the accuracy of these data, many professors—including yours—would likely argue that they are misleading for several reasons. First, they combine information from colleges, universities, and professional schools; junior colleges; technical and trade schools; general medical and surgical hospitals; and business schools and computer and

management training—very different kinds of institutions with very different pay scales. Second, they ignore regional differences: 2011 data from the U.S. Bureau of Statistics show that the average wage in these fields in Massachusetts was $120,170 while for the nonmetropolitan regions of Southeast Iowa, it was $45,760. (Of course, the cost of living in those two locations is quite different as well, but those differences alone would not account for such disparities in wages.) Third, as the Bureau of Labor Statistics Web site notes in a footnote to one of the charts providing data on this topic, the data assume year-round full-time employment though most professors with full-time jobs at four-year institutions have nine-month contracts and, increasingly, institutions use part-time faculty as a cost-saving measure. While other observations could be made, it should be clear that these data, though accurate, are, in some basic sense, misleading or potentially misleading. What does this situation demonstrate about the need to understand thoroughly the context(s) in which statistics you might wish to use in constructing arguments were collected as well as the limitations of those statistics?

This situation is a powerful reminder that even hard evidence and inartistic appeals can be manipulated and misleading.

5–6. Writing assignments

Classroom Exercise: focus on rhetoric

Question 4 reminds us that even hard evidence can tell multiple stories depending on how its interpreted. Building on question 6, ask students to take the paragraph that they have written and then find grounds for disagreement with their own text. That is, they should use the same graph as evidence for an argument that makes not just a different point from their original paragraph, but one that requires an alternative interpretation of the same graph. They can be willfully misleading in their practice paragraph—it might be good practice for understanding how easily we can misread statistical evidence.

Laurence Shatkin *Education Pays, but Perhaps Less Than You Thought* pp. 854–56

1. Take Shatkin's challenge, and Google "education pays." (If the Bureau of Labor Statistics [BLS] isn't the first hit you get, look down the list until you find the most recent BLS statistics on this topic.) How do current data compare with those from 2008? Why,

for Shatkin, are the statistics from the U.S. Bureau of Labor Statistics at least partially misleading? (Be careful here: there is more than one step to the argument.)

First, Shatkin notes that how much people earn is only one way of measuring their overall well-being. Second, he notes that those who earn more tend to live in places where housing costs more, thus negating some of the increases in their income.

2. What might account for the concentration of college graduates in urban areas, according to Enrico Moretti? Which hypothesis does he prefer?

Moretti offers two hypotheses. The first is the "demand-pull hypothesis," which suggests that highly skilled workers go to cities because they are more productive there and job opportunities attract them. The second hypothesis is the "supply-pull hypothesis," which suggests that college graduates want to live in cities because they are attracted to the amenities there and that once they move there they drive rents up. Moretti prefers the demand-pull hypothesis.

The fact that Moretti does not rule out one of the two hypotheses likely means that he does not have adequate data to draw a conclusion. Do you favor one hypothesis over the other on the basis of your life experiences? Which one and why?

Answers will vary.

Why might Moretti, as an economist, not be willing to trust his life experience in answering this question?

Economists are usually trained to study and rely on inartistic proofs for their evidence, so professionally he probably values statistical trends more than personal observations.

3. Does Moretti's study or Shatkin's discussion of taxes mean that the Bureau of Labor Statistics is wrong? Why or why not?

No, the discussion of taxes does not mean that the Bureau of Labor Statistics is wrong, because the Bureau is reporting only the median weekly earnings and not claiming to report net pay after taxes. It does, though, mean that the Bureau of Labor Statistics is reporting only partial information (but that's often true of a statistical report).

4. Chapter 4 discusses statistics as examples of hard evidence or what Aristotle termed "inartistic appeals." What does this selection remind us about the nature and limitations of so-called hard evidence?

Hard evidence can still leave out some information; for example, in this article the fact that those with more education make more money does not address issues such as how far that money goes, how it contributes to quality of life, and so on.

5. Writing assignment

Classroom Exercise: focus on the argument

The results of the research discussed in this reading might trouble some students, especially those who have taken out significant loans to finance their education. What is their education worth to them? What amount would they *not* pay to attend college? What kind of return do they expect on their investment in economic terms? What about in noneconomic measures? What kinds of rewards and benefits do they expect will accompany their college education experience?

Mark Bauerlein *The Major and the Job Market, the Dream and the Reality* pp. 857–58

1. What argument(s) is Bauerlein making?

Bauerlein argues that professors and other advisors need to help students choose majors and career paths that are practical and that will keep students from going deeply into debt.

What sorts of evidence does he offer for the claims he makes?

Bauerlein offers the narrative about Grant's series of choices that led him to massive debt and no job as his primary evidence.

To what degrees are his arguments based on facts and reason? On emotion? On character? (See Chapters 2–4 for discussions of these kinds of arguments.)

Among the possibilities: When Bauerlein bases his argument on the *Occupational Outlook Handbook* or when he cites how much money Grant owes in student loans, he is using facts and reason. When he opens the third paragraph

171

by trying to control our reaction to Grant's choices, Bauerlein is depending on arguments based on emotion. When Bauerlein tells the story of his own undergraduate experience and his own experience as an advisor, he is building his argument based on character; he portrays himself as someone who understands the situations that he is writing about and how to address them.

What is your response to his argument(s)?

Answers will vary.

2. Who is Bauerlein's invoked audience? His intended audience? What is the relationship between them? What evidence can you give for your claims?

Bauerlein invokes an audience of middle-aged readers, those who remember when college was much cheaper. His intended audience is most likely professors and those who advise students in educational settings and, perhaps, secondarily, parents of college-age students. The last paragraph clearly indicates the audience of professors and advisors; the opening anecdote suggests that Bauerlein is trying to develop sympathy with those who are, say, 40 to 60 years old. The article appeared in the *Chronicle of Higher Education*, a publication whose audience consists largely of professors and others who work at colleges and universities.

3. Why might Bauerlein have begun his blog posting with a personal anecdote rather than with the claim that he makes in the opening line of paragraph 2?

Bauerlein builds a bridge with his audience by telling a story about a time when college decisions and financing were very different from today.

Would the posting have been more or less effective if he had begun by clearly stating his position rather than by telling a story?

Answers will vary. We tend to believe it would be less effective to state the position clearly because the opening story sets up a clear contrast from a previous generation.

Why might this anecdote be especially effective given his intended audience? (See Chapter 4 on the value of testimonies and narratives.)

His intended audience may benefit from a reminder that their own experience with making college and career choices happened in a vastly different context from what students experience today.

4. Because of the blog posting's final paragraph, we can easily claim that this selection represents a proposal. What proposal is Bauerlein making?

Bauerlein proposes that professors advise students to think carefully about what occupational fields are growing or are promising and to think consciously about preparing themselves for work.

To what extent is his proposal well developed, according to the criteria given in Chapter 12?

Answers may vary. Bauerlein clearly defines a problem and offers a strong and clear claim, but he does not anticipate many objections (for example, what about students who seem to be certain that they want to pursue a career with a dreary outlook? What advice does a professor give them?). Bauerlein suggests that a choice of major is equivalent to a choice of career, and many audience members may think that he is conflating categories.

Do you believe that Bauerlein's proposal is a judicious one?

Answers will vary.

5. As is not uncommon in blog postings, Bauerlein quotes at length from another source, here an article from the *Los Angeles Times* about the Occupy Wall Street movement, after commenting on it. Why might he have included the passage after he has commented on it?

Bauerlein can influence our reaction to Grant by framing how we should react to him ahead of time. He suggests that we think of him as "a good kid" and not "a whiner."

How would the blog be different if he had quoted the passage first and then commented on it?

Had he quoted first, his audience might have been less inclined to agree with Bauerlein's opinion of Grant, or they might have focused on other ideas altogether.

6. Writing assignment

Classroom Exercise: focus on the argument

In paragraph 3, Bauerlein asks of the student who had accumulated $90,000 in student loan debt, "Had he heard too many 'follow your dreams' and 'pursue your passion' exhortations in high school?" In asking this question, Bauerlein implies that these clichéd pieces of advice are perhaps dangerously misleading. Your students have probably heard this same advice—what do they think? Should we follow our dreams? Should we pursue our passions? How far? To what degree? How can we tell where to draw the line between the practical and the ideal? Ask students to write an informal, reflective piece that evaluates this life advice, and then ask them to discuss what they feel is good advice for making decisions about how to live their lives.

Craig Lambert *Our Unpaid, Extra Shadow Work* pp. 860–62

1. What argument(s) is Lambert making?

   Lambert argues that the decline of service in American retail means that we are actually doing more work than we were before even though we don't usually recognize this "shadow work."

   To what extent are they stated explicitly (that is, in a clear statement), and to what extent are they implicit (that is, implied but never made explicit)?

   We feel that his argument establishing the existence of shadow work is explicit but that his argument that shadow work is a burden (and even potentially dangerous) is more implicit.

2. There is much evidence that Lambert is offering a causal argument, but which of the kinds of causal arguments discussed in the "Understanding Causal Arguments" section of Chapter 11 is it? Once you've decided which kind it is, diagram that

argument using the diagrams in this section of Chapter 11 as a model.

We would suggest that Lambert offers a causal argument that is a series of links: the increased use of machines leads to more shadow work which leads to a higher incidence of exhaustion and fatigue in the modern world.

3. Lambert is especially effective in the way that he creates and uses definitions. Not only does he use them to define a term in a specific way, but he also uses them to advance the argument he is making. Examine in detail how he defines "shadow work" (paragraph 2), "subsistence economy" (paragraph 3), and "wetware" (paragraph 12). How does each of these definitions serve to help Lambert's readers understand a key concept while advancing his argument?

Shadow work—with this term Lambert redefines what we may have thought of as a convenience (such as self-checkout at the grocery store) as a burden.

Subsistence economy—with this term Lambert separates us from a way of organizing society that is very different but also a way of life that he later implies we seem to be mimicking.

Wetware—Lambert's alternative term for a brain aligns human beings with robots even as it reminds us of how different we are from robots.

4. Another characteristic of this selection is its ample use of examples as evidence. Take two or three paragraphs of the essay that contain examples you find particularly convincing or interesting, make a list of all the examples that occur in these paragraphs, and determine the specific function for which Lambert uses them. Would the essay have been less convincing with fewer examples? With more examples? How can a writer determine how many examples are needed to create a persuasive argument?

Answers will vary. One thing you might discuss with students is that some concerns outside of a writer's control, such as word limits, will affect any decisions about how many examples to include.

5. Writing assignment

Ask students to interrogate the definition of "shadow work" by having them keep track of how many things they do in a two- or three-day span that can be categorized as shadow work. Are they surprised by how much of their lives are devoted to "menial, repetitive tasks" (paragraph 6)? Has Lambert accurately described the world that they live in or is this a misleading definition that he has proposed? Does shadow work disconnect them from aspects of a human community (as Lambert suggests might happen in paragraph 15)?

Thomas L. Friedman *"The Start-Up of You" and Readers'*
Responses pp. 864–69

1. What arguments is Friedman making?

   Friedman argues that old career models are no longer applicable in the current economy and that all workers need to think of themselves as entrepreneurs rather than as employees.

   What consequences might these arguments have for you as you think about your future in the workplace, whether you plan to work in the United States or internationally?

   Answers will vary.

2. Before what is often termed Web 2.0—the version of the Internet we are all familiar with now, one that encourages participation by permitting users to post comments, photos, and videos; create blogs; and interact with other users in novel ways—newspapers encouraged debate by publishing letters to the editor on their editorial pages: a few selected letters appeared, generally offering a limited range of responses to the original article. Obviously, the commenting function so common in Web 2.0 has changed the nature of responding to arguments publicly since anyone with Internet access and the desire to do so can respond—and frequently they do. One tip for how to learn about the complexity of a topic and the range of opinions surrounding it is to read the comments posted about an article on the topic in papers like *New York Times*. (In smaller papers, the comments sections often become shouting matches full of snarky comments that provide little or no evidence for the claims made. For whatever reasons, readers of the *Times* generally provide at least some evidence for

their claims.) Study the letters and comments reprinted in this selection, noting the number of people who support Friedman's argument(s) in some way and those who are critical of them or some part of them. Be sure to note down the evidence offered by those who support or critique his positions.

Answers will vary.

3. Once you have completed question 2, turn your attention to those who critique Friedman's position in particular. In many cases, their critiques assume or claim that Friedman has made faulty assumptions or has committed some of the fallacies of argument discussed in Chapter 5. (After all, making faulty assumptions can generally be analyzed as evidence of fallacious thinking.) Which particular fallacies might they claim Friedman has engaged in? Which category of fallacy—those of emotional argument, ethical argument, or logical argument—do these fall into?

Answers may vary. A few suggestions are provided below:

Comment 8 from C Wolfe suggests that Friedman has engaged in the emotional fallacy of the bandwagon effect by joining with those who believe that social networking companies have actual value.

Comment 26 from harry and Comment 64 from Hi USA suggest that Friedman has engaged in the fallacies of ethical argument of dogmatism or stacking the deck because he does not consider models of the economy other than the one that he has put forward in his article.

Comment 170 from David Andrews and Comment 206 from Sharon Reagan suggest that Friedman has engaged in the logical fallacy of hasty generalization by describing economic life for a small number of Americans rather than for most Americans.

4. Comment 206 by Sharon Reagan could be tweeted. Would it be an effective argument as a tweet?

Answers may vary; we would point out that the parallel structure in this tweet helps make the sentence more effective as an argument. On the other hand, the small slip of

not including a question mark at the end might bother some readers as a lack of attention to detail.

What are some of the features of an effective tweet?

In the limited space of a tweet, writing style takes on more importance; well-crafted tweets need to accomplish a great deal in a small space. Tweets also benefit from being properly marked: hashtags allow an author to enter a conversation or debate without needing to provide other context.

How do tweets differ rhetorically from longer arguments of the sorts represented by the other comments posted here?

Tweets do not have the space to cite evidence to build the argument. Tweets tend to be mostly claim, with fewer reasons than longer arguments.

5. Not surprisingly, several of the posted comments address the same issue—that is, they offer the same support for or criticism of Friedman's position. Working with a classmate, choose a group of comments (including one of the letters if you like) that take a similar position, and determine which is most effective and why.

   Answers will vary.

6. Writing assignment

Classroom Exercise: focus on the argument

Build on question 5 by having students discuss fallacies of argument across the comments in this reading, with a particular focus on Comment 279 from DK. Does this comment cross the line into an *ad hominem* attack or is it justified? How do we sort out what constitutes a fallacy and what constitutes a legitimate argument? Can students find other examples of difficult-to-categorize claims that may be fallacies in the comments?

Stewart D. Friedman *The Fallacy of "Work-Life Balance"*   pp. 871–72

Take the Four-Way View pp. 873–74

1. What argument is Stewart D. Friedman making in the video that is excerpted on the Amazon.com Web site? In what ways is it a definitional argument? (In addition to the features of definition

argument discussed in Chapter 9, note that a common strategy in a definitional argument is saying what something is *not*, as Friedman does here.)

Friedman argues that "balance" is the wrong metaphor for figuring out how to live our lives. By rejecting the metaphor of balance, Friedman attempts to redefine how we think about our lives.

How is ethos created in this short video? (Consider not only what is said but also how it is packaged.)

First, the logo for Harvard Business Publishing, which opens the video and stays in the corner throughout the presentation, associates the author with a prestigious academic institution. Second, his suit and the formal background create an air of seriousness. Third, his academic tone and the precision of his speech help establish a sense of expertise.

2. Focus on the structure of the chapter from *Total Leadership*. (You may wish to list the titles of the sections and exercises in the order in which they occur to help you analyze the chapter's structure.) To what extent and in what ways is this chapter organized according to the principles of stasis theory (which are discussed in Chapter 1) or the categories of argument that are presented in the text (arguments of fact, arguments of definition, arguments of evaluation, causal arguments, and proposals)?

Friedman opens the chapter by referring to the previous chapter, which asked readers to recognize the fact of the four domains. In the next section he instructs readers to define the domains. After that, he asks readers to evaluate how their attention to different domains fits their values and to investigate why (causes) their lives are ordered as they are now. The end of the chapter could be read as a proposal argument for reshaping one's life according to the values clarified by the exercise.

Why is such an organization appropriate, given Friedman's goals?

Friedman wants to move his readers through a process and to propose to readers a new way of imagining their lives, so he needs to move them through the steps of stasis theory to establish the problem and find a solution for it.

3. How does Friedman use the extended examples of Victor and Roxanne to advance his argument?

We might think of them as emotional arguments: reading about how actual people experience the steps that Friedman recommends allows us to connect the goals of the program with our own lives as we recognize similar struggles to allocate our time and energy.

Would his argument be less effective without these examples? Why? What specific roles do they play in the argument?

Answers will vary, though we suggest that without the examples the argument would feel too abstract.

4. What role do the activities in the chapter play in Friedman's argument?

The activities encourage readers to participate in the reading and to develop their own arguments about what's happening in their own lives.

What did you learn from doing them, for example? (If you didn't complete them, do so now.)

Answers will vary.

How are these activities indicated in the text?

They are set off with a different typography and a box that marks them as separate from the rest of the text.

How effective is the layout of the text in this regard?

Answers will vary.

What roles do Figures 3-1 and 3-2 play in Friedman's argument? What are the benefits of including two such figures, rather than simply relying on one?

These figures help readers see how to create their own responses, and the differences between them help readers understand that there's not only one way to graph this information.

5. Writing assignment

Classroom Exercise: focus on the argument

Friedman argues that the metaphor of balance is not a good one for thinking about our lives. Have students brainstorm other metaphors for their lives. For example, some critics say that Homer's epic poems, the *Iliad* and the *Odyssey*, set out two primary metaphors for our lives, life as a battle and life as a journey. What other metaphors can students come up with to describe their lives? Ask them to write a definition argument in which they defend a particular metaphor as being especially useful for thinking about their lives.

Wrap-up Exercises for "What Are You Working For?"

1. What does your ideal work life look like? How does it balance work and leisure, what sorts of rewards (not just financial) does it offer, and what kind of preparation does it require? For this evaluative argument, be sure that you use the tools provided by Toulmin logic—carefully defend your claim with adequate evidence, warrants, and backing.

2. What does work teach? What *should* we learn from working? What *do* we learn from working—is it always positive? That is, can some kinds of work teach lessons that we might regret learning? Based on your own experience and/or the experiences of those you know and interview, write an essay that takes a position on the lessons afforded by work, however you wish to define it.

3. Using the evidence provided by the readings in this chapter, write an essay in which you make a claim for how your school should prepare students for their working lives. Should your school teach students how to think about how work fits into the rest of one's life, as Stewart Friedman does? Should your school prepare workers for a world where their home and work lives will intersect seamlessly? Should your school not worry about preparing people for work at all but instead focus on a broad education that emphasizes skills and thinking?

CHAPTER 27

How Do We Define "Inequality" in American Society?

The Occupy Wall Street protests brought the idea of economic inequality to the forefront of American attention in the fall and winter of 2011. But the protests raised as many questions as they answered, and those questions led to the rich selection of readings in this chapter. One aspect of this chapter that instructors may find especially useful is the tight focus of the readings. Because of this focus, students can probably identify the stases in arguments about inequality fairly easily. For example:

- Arguments of fact: Is inequality increasing in the United States?
- Arguments of definition: What do we mean by "inequality"? Are there other, more important ways of thinking about what we mean by inequality that can't be captured by economics?
- Arguments of evaluation: Does economic inequality hurt Americans? If so, how much?
- Causal arguments: What are the effects of income inequality? Did it cause the financial crisis of the last few years and can it cause a greater financial crisis if it continues? If it is rising, why? If not, why do so many people think it is?
- Proposal arguments: What, if anything, shall we do about income inequality?

For some students, especially middle- and upper-middle-class students who have not often thought about the idea that their economic situation could ever be negative, this chapter might be one that elicits strong disagreement or even resistance to entertaining opposing views. Fortunately, the chapter and, of course, the book as a whole are committed to the idea that there are many valid perspectives on any viewpoint—as long as there's an argument to back up the idea.

Richard Morin, Pew Research Center *Rising Share of Americans See Conflict between Rich and Poor*   pp. 888–99

1. What was your response to this information? Was it old news to you? Did any of the findings surprise you? If so, which ones and why? How aware were you of the changes that have taken place in American attitudes toward these issues over the past decades?

   Answers will vary.

2. Why do the authors of this report give the wording of the question that those interviewed responded to? (Pay special attention to footnotes 4 and 5 here.)

   Giving the wording of the question shows that the authors recognize that *how* they ask the question can influence the response that a survey participant gives; by showing their commitment to fairness, the authors attempt to create a trustworthy ethos.

   In what other ways do the authors demonstrate that they are seeking to create an ethos of trustworthiness?

   The authors frequently limit and/or qualify their claims and arguments (see, for example, the first sentence of paragraph 9), and they place their data in context so that readers have points of comparison. Further, the endnotes clearly document their research and explain their research methods.

3. Evaluate the visual arguments in this report. How effective are they? Consider them from two perspectives that are often used to evaluation visual arguments. First, can each chart stand alone? (That is, can you understand each chart without reading the accompanying text?) Second, is the relationship between the chart and the text that comments on it clear and easy to follow? Finally, consider a third question: Would the figures and text have worked better together if the authors had labeled each figure with a number (e.g., Figure 1, Figure 2, etc.) and referred to the chart by the number in the text, as is required by the style manual of the American Psychological Association? Why or why not?

   Answers will vary.

4–5. Writing assignments.

As the headnote mentions, this report garnered national headlines, but one of the unresolved issues in the piece might be what constitutes "class conflict." How does the article define this term? How do you define this term? Can you locate other terms in this report that need additional definition or clarification? (It might be useful to read Andrew Kohut's "Don't Mind the Gap" alongside this piece to make the issues at stake in this question more apparent.)

Rana Foroohar *What Ever Happened to Upward Mobility?*   pp. 901–8

1. Clearly, Foroohar assumes that the situation Americans find themselves in is a complex one that is best understood by thinking historically and thinking comparatively, that is, by comparing the United States to other countries around the world. What does each perspective contribute to her causal argument?

   In terms of historical context, Foroohar argues that great social mobility has long been a key American value but that the actual opportunity for social mobility has slowed for current generations. In terms of comparison to European countries, Foroohar suggests that the United States has to wrestle with the issues created by greater diversity, which makes social mobility more difficult. Paragraphs 15–19 argue that greater public spending on social welfare and social safety nets actually improves social mobility. Paragraphs 20 and 21 suggest that European tax codes improve social mobility, economic stability, and the overall health of the society (and even individuals).

   To your understanding of issues of inequality in the United States?

   Answers will vary.

2. Among the things that Foroohar does well as a writer is to give her readers background information in places where they might need it, whether in terms of definitions or short descriptions that give readers a context for interpreting claims she is making. In

what specific ways does she define or describe each of the following terms or things?

- absolute mobility (paragraph 5)

  She defines absolute mobility as "the extent to which people are better off than their parents were at the same age," which she says is basically a measure of how much economic growth has taken place.

- relative mobility (paragraph 6)

  She explains that relative mobility takes into account the idea that "our sense of well-being is tied not to the past but to how we are doing compared with our peers."

- Opportunity Nation (paragraph 10)

  Foorohar defines Opportunity Nation as "a coalition of private and public institutions dedicated to increasing social mobility."

- McKinsey Global Institute (paragraph 13)

  Foorohar describes the McKinsey Global Institute as one of the "advocates of technology-driven economic growth."

- New American Foundation (paragraph 13)

  Foorohar introduces the New American Foundation as "a public-policy think tank."

Why is this information useful and perhaps even necessary?

Foroohar makes a complicated argument that suggests that a prized American value does not seem to matter; this is an argument many American readers are likely to reject or want to reject. Were she to leave out explanations of some of these details and sources, readers would be less likely to trust her.

3. Another skill Foroohar has mastered is the ability to move between levels of generality within a paragraph. Thus, most paragraphs begin with a generalization or topic sentence and then

become more specific before moving on to make a point in support of her argument. Analyze paragraphs 8 and 17 in this regard, explaining what Foroohar does to move from more general to more specific. In other words, how does she use specific forms of evidence to shift from general claim to more specific support for that claim?

In paragraph 8, Foroohar begins with a general claim that Europe encourages equality more than the United States. She then argues that high inequality correlates to lower mobility, and she ends by explaining that American inequality now is as high as it was during the Gilded Age.

In paragraph 17, Foroohar begins with a general claim about the effects of higher spending on social safety nets and then moves into the example of technical schools and job training programs and ends by explaining that when teenagers are not in school or working, there is less mobility.

Choose a third paragraph you find interesting, and comment on it from this perspective.

Answers will vary.

4. Writing assignment

Classroom Exercise: focus on the argument

How central to American identity is the idea of social mobility? Frequently social mobility is cited as being equivalent to the American dream, as it is in this article, but that doesn't mean social mobility *must* be the key idea. What constitutes the American dream for you? Is there still such an idea as the American dream? If so, what does it look like? How accessible is it for you? For the average American? For poor Americans?

Jim Harper *Tea Party, Meet Occupy Wall Street. OWS, Tea Party.* pp. 909–10

1. Summarize the argument James Sinclair is making in his visual argument, and summarize the argument Jim Harper, who is responsible for this reposting on the Cato Institute blog, is making in his contextualization of Sinclair's argument.

Sinclair argues that Tea Partiers and the Occupy Wall Street protesters actually share quite a bit of common ground in their beliefs. Jim Harper argues that Sinclair's argument has significant merit and that libertarians and conservatives should not be too quick to reject the OWS movement, or the Tea Party movement, as a result.

2. Who is Harper's intended audience?

Harper's intended audience is composed of libertarians and libertarian-leaning conservatives who might reject the Occupy Wall Street movement at first.

His invoked audience? How can you use specific comments in the text, including the items that we felt we needed to gloss, as evidence for claims about Harper's intended and invoked audiences?

Harper invokes an audience of libertarians in the first paragraph when he talks about ideological purity and even refers to libertarians as "we." He invokes an older audience—perhaps not old enough really to remember the 1960s but old enough to recognize what "Kent State" and "dirty hippies" and "drum circle" represent in the culture, and old enough to feel that the OWS movement might be a throwback to a different age.

3. Examine the way that Sinclair contextualized his own visual argument by reading the blog posting in which it originally appeared in "Occupy Wall Street vs. The Tea Party" at http://bit.ly/oHPX6B as well as a later posting about responses to the diagram reproduced here, "Bringing America Together, One Venn Diagram at a Time" at http://bit.ly/oHPX6B. (By the way, *cromulent* in the latter posting means "fine," and our online dictionary labels it as slang. We had to look it up, so we thought you might need to know its meaning too.) What was Sinclair trying to do with the original diagram? What was his motivation for creating the visual argument?

Sinclair uses the diagram to illustrate the similarities that he was explaining between the Tea Party and the Occupy movement. His motivation was to make the argument simple to follow.

Does it appear that he succeeded? Why or why not?

Answers will vary, though the comments suggest very positive reactions from many readers.

Could we consider Sinclair's diagram a case of Rogerian argumentation? Why or why not?

Yes, Sinclair's diagram (and blog post as a whole) could be considered a case of Rogerian argument because it seeks to find the common ground between two points of view that had commonly been taken to be so strongly in opposition to each other that they could never find agreement.

4. As the title of one of his blog postings notes (see question 3), Sinclair contends that Venn diagrams are very useful in thinking through complex problems. What advantages can you see to using visual arguments like the one Sinclair presents? If you haven't read the posting "Bringing America Together, One Venn Diagram at a Time" at http://bit.ly/oHPX6B (mentioned in question 3), do so now, and explain what Sinclair thinks the advantages of such diagrams are in understanding issues and creating arguments.

Sinclair argues that the primary advantage of such a visual argument is simplicity, particularly the simplicity of pointing out problems without being responsible for identifying or implementing solutions.

5. Writing assignment

Classroom Exercise: focus on the world

Sinclair intends to bring together two disparate groups who normally disagree. Can you think of other arguments in the political arena where groups who seem to disagree are far closer than we normally think them to be? Alternatively, are there alliances in modern politics that don't make sense to you? Where do you see two groups finding unexpected common ground, or where do you think that two groups could find unexpected common ground?

John Marsh *Why Education Is Not an Economic Panacea* pp. 912–19

1. What arguments is Marsh making about the relationship between inequality and education in the United States?

Marsh argues that more education will not correct the problem of inequality because a lack of education did not create the problem of inequality. He then goes on to argue that decreasing poverty and inequality might be the first step for improving education outcomes.

How does he distinguish his position from other common arguments about the degree to which education, especially higher education, can or cannot serve as a panacea for social ills in this or other countries?

Marsh presents his argument as a counter to the conventional wisdom that more education will reduce inequality. In paragraphs 26 and 27 Marsh explains the differences between his own argument and those of Charles Murray, Richard Vedder, and Matthew B. Crawford, three other writers who have argued that "college for all" will not really benefit the United States.

2. What evidence does Marsh offer for his argument?

Marsh offers evidence from his experience directing the Odyssey Project as well as background on the history of land-grant institutions in the United States, and statistical evidence about salaries for different levels of education.

Can you restate his argument, including the evidence, in the form of a Toulmin argument as discussed in Chapter 7?

Answers will vary. One possibility:

Claim: Americans should quit believing that education will eliminate economic inequality because education alone cannot play that role.

Evidence:

Eliminating economic inequality should be our goal, but it will require many other steps besides education.

Economic inequality runs counter to American values.

Eliminating economic inequality is a complicated, multifaceted process.

3. How convincing is the evidence Marsh offers for his argument? Why? What criteria can you use in evaluating the evidence he of-

fers? How might readers with different value commitments evaluate his evidence? Why?

Answers will vary.

What are the advantages and disadvantages of relying heavily on personal experience as evidence in the way that Marsh does?

Marsh's argument is especially powerful because of his personal experience. His heavy involvement with the program followed by his turn to doubt of the program makes his argument especially effective. On the other hand, we never learn of any statistics of how education does or does not help people out of poverty, nor do we hear stories about how the participants might have been affected, so the focus on his experience feels somewhat limited.

4. This essay, based largely on personal experience, uses a common trope or figure of speech not discussed in Chapter 6, specifically, *protrepticus*, or "turning," specifically, a change of one's path (see especially paragraphs 15–24). This trope is, of course, found in all conversion narratives, whether the change involves accepting a new religion or rejecting an old one. What triggers Marsh's turning?

The conversation he has with the television reporter just before his interview: after the reporter says that more education would solve "all these problems" (paragraph 14), Marsh realizes that education cannot solve all of the problems but that it's convenient for Americans to think so.

How reasonable is it that someone with his life experience would never have entertained the doubts he comes to entertain?

Answers may vary, but someone who dedicates his or her life to a particular profession is likely to find reasons to defend and not question that profession, as Marsh seems to have done for several years. Further, as the article suggests, not many forces in popular culture (until, perhaps, recently) speak against education—in many arguments, education *is* a panacea.

What might the fact that he had not entertained these doubts tell us about the power of the set of beliefs he comes to question?

His reluctance to embrace those doubts reminds us that we take many ideas for granted and that these ideas exert an extremely powerful hold over us.

5. Writing assignment

Classroom Exercise: focus on the argument

Marsh argues that education is not a panacea; how, then, might we articulate the value of education? What, if anything, makes education valuable? Is there a value to education that is not easily measured in economic terms? Based on what you learned from the article, is there any good defense of the Odyssey Project beyond the positive publicity for the school? Is there any evidence that the students received anything of value?

Making a Visual Argument: Inequality and the Occupy Movement pp. 921–25

1. What argument is each of the Occupy George dollar bills making?

The first Occupy George bill argues that the 400 richest Americans control the same amount of wealth as the bottom 50% of the entire country.

The second Occupy George bill argues that the current growth in income disparity is greater than it was in the 1920s and far greater than it was in the 1960s.

The third Occupy George bill argues that the average CEO makes 185 times as much as the average worker.

The fourth Occupy George bill argues that the top 1% controls about 33% of the wealth in the United States and that the bottom 80% control under 20% of the wealth; the rest is in the hands of about a fifth of the population, who themselves control a great deal of wealth.

The fifth Occupy George bill argues that the stamped dollar bill will ultimately belong to the top 1% as, presumably, most dollar bills will.

Why might supporters have chosen dollar bills as the medium with which to make their arguments?

Among the many reasons students might cite: dollar bills underscore that the Occupy Movement is making arguments about money; dollar bills circulate widely, so the message stamped on them will be seen by many people (even people who resist the arguments will want to get hold of the dollar bills); dollar bills are a standard size, so the movement can create a template; it's more practical to print these messages on the more readily available dollar bills than on, say, one hundred dollar bills.

2. Visit the Occupy George Web site (occupygeorge.com). How do the statements presented there help make the visual arguments printed in this section more concrete?

The statements are extremely simple without dramatic stylistic flourishes; combined with the availability of a source for all of the statistics, the statements make the visual arguments seem grounded in facts.

How would you characterize the argument made by the Web site in terms of the arguments described in Chapters 8–12? In other words, what kinds of arguments are they? What evidence can you cite for your claims?

The arguments are primarily arguments of fact; most of the arguments claim that certain income disparities exist. The dollar bills also strongly imply evaluation arguments, as they encourage us to see these inequalities as bad for the country (see especially bill number 2, where the explanation compares the current situation to the period just before the Great Depression).

3. What are the similarities and differences in the images involving pepper spray? What arguments do these images make?

All three images emphasize the harshness of pepper spray; in fact, these images suggest police brutality, though in different ways. The Portland photo makes the police seem brutal, but the UC–Davis photo makes the police seem to be *casually* brutal; that is, the picture makes it seem as if there is no reason at all for the attack. The Seattle photo emphasizes the effects on a human of a pepper spray attack.

Which is most effective in making its argument? Why?

Answers will vary.

Why might such images provoke a great deal of debate in American society?

Seeing images of Americans being pepper sprayed—especially an elderly woman or people who seem to be sitting and protesting peacefully—may conjure up images of police brutality and make America look like a totalitarian state. Americans generally like to believe that our country tolerates dissent and debate especially well, but these pictures do not support that image. On the other hand, many Americans are frustrated by the Occupy Movement and feel that the protestors need to take a shower and get a job, so they may be more sympathetic to police frustration and feel that the pepper sprayings could be justified.

Should they? Why or why not?

Answers will vary.

4. Visit the Web site of We Are the 99% (wearthe99percent.us). How would you characterize the arguments made by the Web site in terms of the arguments described in Chapters 8–12? What evidence can you cite for your claim?

These arguments are primarily arguments of fact, with evaluation arguments strongly implied. The dependence on short statements that are mostly statistics provides strong evidence for the idea that the arguments are mostly factual.

Do different parts of the Web site function as different kinds of argument?

While most of the site offers arguments of fact, the Links section offers links to several proposal arguments and the Reads section contains links to longer arguments that include definition, evaluation, cause, and proposal arguments.

What does the Occupy movement assume about the power of such arguments?

The Occupy movement seems to assume that arguments of fact will be enough to convince many people to get involved in the movement. Both the Occupy George site and this site offer relatively few causal or proposal arguments (beyond the broad proposal to become part of the movement), and the evaluation arguments are largely implied.

5. Writing assignment

Classroom Exercise: focus on the argument

How effective do you find the Occupy George protests? What effect does putting these messages on dollar bills have on you? Do you think that you're likely to take these arguments more or less seriously because of their placement on currency? What about arguments made in other nontraditional places, such as arguments spray-painted onto buildings or stop signs? How do you react to those arguments? Think about a topic of interest to you: what nontraditional places and methods could you use to make your arguments?

Jonathan Chait *Steve Jobs, Occupy Wall Street, and the Capitalist Ideal* pp. 927–30

1. What argument is Chait making about Occupy Wall Street at this point in the movement's history, that is, early October 2011?

Chait argues that Occupy Wall Street runs the risk of falling into a narrow, socialist view that rejects all of capitalism as a result of objecting to the worst aspects of capitalism.

What argument is he making about conservative thinkers like Mitt Romney and Kevin Williamson?

Chait argues that Romney and Williamson are the mirror images of the socialists who reject capitalism outright; they see the issue as all-or-nothing and embrace capitalism without recognizing its shortcomings, which Chait thinks can be regulated.

How would you summarize Chait's position with respect to the issues he discusses?

Chait hopes to see the movement adopt a position of regulated capitalism; he wants to forge a middle way between

those who reject capitalism for its faults and those who suggest that capitalism has no faults.

2. How does Chait carve out a space for his position by pointing out what he sees as the shortcomings of others' positions? Point to specific places in the text where he does this.

Paragraphs 3 and 4 argue that Chait's position is between two all-or-nothing extremes. Paragraph 5 clearly separates Chait from the "Marxist drivel" of some of the Occupy protestors, while paragraphs 7 and 8 point out the shortcomings of the conservative position, arguing that Williamson falls into an "analytic trap" and that Williamson basically misunderstands his own position.

3. Chait mentions Romney's use of a metaphor involving iPhones and pay phones. Unpack this metaphor; that is, explain exactly what two things are being compared literally and metaphorically. Why might Romney speak of a "pay phone strategy" instead of, say, a "land-line strategy"?

Romney might use a "pay phone strategy" because pay phones seem particularly outdated. Those payphones that still exist are often inconvenient and not well cared for, while land lines are still common and even, in a few cases such as after storms or other natural disasters, more reliable than cell phones. Further, calling attention to pay phones would remind listeners that Romney wants to focus attention on how Obama will tax them and cost them money.

How effective do you find this metaphor? What are its limits or limitations?

Answers may vary. One limitation is that pay phones are so outdated that associating Obama with them may not make sense to some audiences; another limitation is that by associating himself with iPhones, Romney may remind audiences of his own wealth.

4. Like many bloggers, Chait is quick to use lengthy quotations from other sources and to make his point by using sarcasm and humor. How effective are these practices in blogging? Why?

195

Answers will vary, though the more conversational tone of blogging probably makes these practices relatively effective.

Why are they generally less effective—or even impermissible—in academic writing?

The conventions of academic writing demand more seriousness.

5. Writing assignment

Classroom Exercise: focus on rhetoric

What changes would you make to rewrite Chait's blog posting as a more academic argument? Working with a classmate, choose a paragraph or two to rewrite as an academic essay. What does Chait already do to achieve an academic tone? What aspects did you have to change to make the argument more academic?

Mac McClelland *Goodbye, Columbus: Ohio's War on the Middle Class* pp. 931–42

1. How would you summarize McClelland's argument?

   McClelland argues that the current economic situation in Ohio is dire: even the well educated struggle to find work, those who find work have to struggle to make ends meet, and the government policy that the state is currently pursuing will likely hurt the working and middle classes.

   Can you likewise summarize the kinds of evidence she provides to support it?

   McClelland's evidence consists largely of personal narratives from people in their thirties.

   Do you believe that "[her] generation is flat-out screwed," a question raised in the selection's introduction?

   Answers will vary.

2. Rather than stating an argument explicitly, McClelland tells a series of interlocking stories. Which of the stories (or strands of a story) do you find most effective? Why? Which do you find least compelling? Why? Are they all necessary? Why or why not?

   Answers will vary.

3. As noted, McClelland recounts a series of stories rather than making an explicit argument. What are the advantages and disadvantages of using such a technique when constructing an argument? To what extent is the evidence for her argument the cumulative weight of all the stories she tells?

Stories make for compelling reading, and they guarantee that arguments won't feel overly abstract so that readers can identify with what's being described. However, it can be hard to know how typical a few selected stories really are, and some audiences might dismiss a narrative argument as the stories of only a few people and therefore unpersuasive.

4. Examine this article as it originally appeared online at http://bit .ly/qrnrrG, paying special attention to the photos that are part of the layout as well as their captions. Choose two that you think are especially effective in supporting McClelland's argument. Be prepared to explain your choices to your classmates.

   Answers will vary.

5–6. Writing assignments

Classroom Exercise: focus on the world

To what degree do you feel like a member of your generation? What are your generation's defining characteristics, and how well do you fit into them? How much of your identity can be attributed to sociological factors outside of your experience of yourself? (You may need to do some research to see how sociologists and others write about your generation; indeed, you may need to do some research to figure out which generation you even fit into if you don't normally think of yourself as part of a particular generation.)

Andrew Kohut *Don't Mind the Gap*   pp. 945–46

1. What is Kohut's argument in this selection?

   Kohut argues that the Pew Research Center's poll indicates that a strong majority of Americans want "the government to increase opportunities for people to get ahead" (paragraph 11).

   As Kohut notes, the Pew Research Center's poll on income inequality, which was the first selection in this chapter, "Rising

Share of Americans See Conflict between Rich and Poor," received "an extraordinary amount of attention." Do you think Kohut believed the poll merited the attention it received? Why or why not?

We would suggest that Kohut believes the poll received the wrong kind of attention and that people read more meaning into it than they should have. The simple fact that he's writing this article suggests that he wants to argue for a different way of interpreting the poll, and the content of his essay focuses on contextualizing the poll and offering an argument about how he thinks the poll should be understood.

2. How does Kohut go about contextualizing the findings of the poll that served as the first selection in the chapter?

Kohut points out that the results are not that different from polls dating back to as early as 1941 (paragraph 3) and argues that the polls indicate dissatisfaction with tax policy rather than dissatisfaction with inequality itself.

What can his essay teach us about the ways statistical information, including polls, can be used to support very different arguments?

His essay is a reminder that inartistic appeals are not neutral; they can be interpreted to advance the arguments that people want to make.

3. Throughout this essay, Kohut relies most strongly on inartistic arguments, specifically, data from opinion surveys, as evidence. Choose two paragraphs that contain statistical data and analyze carefully how Kohut presents the information in such a way as to support his larger point. As you will note, he doesn't merely drop statistics in, he uses them strategically. What you're trying to get a feel for is how researchers who rely on quantitative date do so effectively.

Answers will vary.

4. Now take one of the paragraphs you analyzed in question 3 and present it as a Toulmin argument, as discussed in Chapter 7. Pay careful attention to the inartistic and artistic arguments (as dis-

cussed in Chapter 4) that Kohut uses in the paragraph you analyze.

Answers will vary.

5. Writing assignment

Classroom Exercise: focus on rhetoric

This piece is an argument about how to read statistics, but Kohut is not necessarily the final authority on the right way to interpret these statistics. Because one of the essential skills of academic argument is the ability to disagree productively, after reading this article carefully, choose a claim that you can disagree with or qualify and write a practice paragraph based on this disagreement or qualification. Sketch an outline for a fuller argument that follows the logic of your claim. Could you write a full essay by qualifying Kohut's claims? What other steps would you need to take?

Stanley Fish *Fair Is Fair*   pp. 948–49

1. Why does Fish argue that emphasizing fairness rather than equality is a more astute way to frame debates about social inequality in the United States?

   Fish argues that fairness is the quality that is more in line with American values and ways of thinking about income inequality; equality is a word that conjures up ideas that Americans are not comfortable with, such as redistribution of income.

   What evidence does he offer?

   Most of Fish's evidence is artistic; he makes generalizations about American values.

   To what extent do you agree or disagree with Fish? Why?

   Answers will vary.

2. What distinction does Fish draw between "formal equality" and "substantive equality"?

   Fish defines "formal equality" as the idea that everyone should have the same rules and that "everyone should be treated alike." "Substantive equality" he defines as eco-

199

nomic equality or the idea that everyone "should have the same stuff."

Why is it important to his argument?

Fish is attempting to explain how Americans think about equality, and he needs to establish definitions that explain how the idea of equality can be thought of in different ways. Further, he needs to establish which definition is popular with Americans.

To what extent do you agree with this distinction? With the ways that Fish uses it?

Answers will vary.

3. In paragraph 4, Fish uses an extended example to illustrate the distinction between equality and fairness. How effective is this example? Why? What can you learn from this paragraph about how to provide effective examples that help clarify the definitions of terms?

Answers will vary, though we would suggest that using this example puts the argument of the previous paragraph into more concrete terms and makes the distinction between formal and substantive equality much easier to understand.

4. In many ways, Fish is offering a proposal argument (see Chapter 12), contending that one way of framing the issue—fairness—is ultimately more effective than framing the issue another way—equality. Which way of framing the issue(s) is more appropriate when the topic is the subject of this chapter—how we define inequality in this society? (You may wish to propose a third way of framing the issues.)

Answers will vary.

5. What are the similarities and differences between Fish's argument and the argument offered by Andrew Kohut in the previous selection, "Don't Mind the Gap"? Pay attention not only to the content of the argument but to the use of artistic and inartistic evidence, as discussed in Chapter 4, as well.

Both arguments reject the idea of class warfare, describing it as bad political strategy, but Fish relies almost entirely on

artistic appeals as evidence whereas Kohut depends on in-artistic appeals, especially numbers drawn from Pew Research Center polls.

6. Writing assignment

Classroom Exercise: focus on rhetoric

Fish's argument is about how to frame the argument, not what he believes is true or right. What do you think about that kind of political argument? Is it less honest or sincere than someone who argues passionately about their beliefs? Historically, rhetoric has often been dismissed as somewhat dishonest. Having studied rhetoric in your use of this book, what do you think of that claim? Is it possible to view rhetoric as fundamentally dishonest?

Wrap-up Exercises for "How Do We Define 'Inequality' in American Society?"

1. Write an essay in which you describe your place in American socioeconomic life. If you're tempted to write about yourself as middle class, consider talking to your family and researching the statistics to try to locate yourself more precisely—upper middle? lower middle? right at the mean for income? How does inequality affect you? Can you locate its effects in your life? If so, or if not, discuss how your feelings of experiencing or not experiencing inequality affect your views on how we should think about the issue in terms of politics. If you're not American, what do you think about American ideas of equality? How are they like or unlike your native country's ideas about equality and income distribution?

2. Write a proposal argument about how the United States should approach the issue of inequality. Use the stases to build your argument: make sure that it's clear what definition of inequality you're using, and use causal and evaluative arguments to help justify your proposal. Of course, it's a perfectly acceptable proposal argument to say that we don't need to do anything, but you'll need to develop that argument as surely as you would the development of a new policy initiative.